Scotland in Dark Age Britain

published 1996
Scottish Cultural Press
PO Box 106, Aberdeen AB9 8ZE
Tel: 01224 583777 • Fax: 01224 575337

British Library Cataloguing in Publication Data
A catalogue record for this book is available from the British Library

ISBN: 1 898218 61 7

Price £9.00.

Designed and typeset by Reprographic Services,
University of St Andrews

Printed and bound by BPC-AUP Aberdeen Ltd

Scotland in Dark Age Britain

The Proceedings of a Day Conference
held on 18 February 1995

Edited by
Barbara E. Crawford

ST ANDREWS
St John's House Papers No. 6
1996

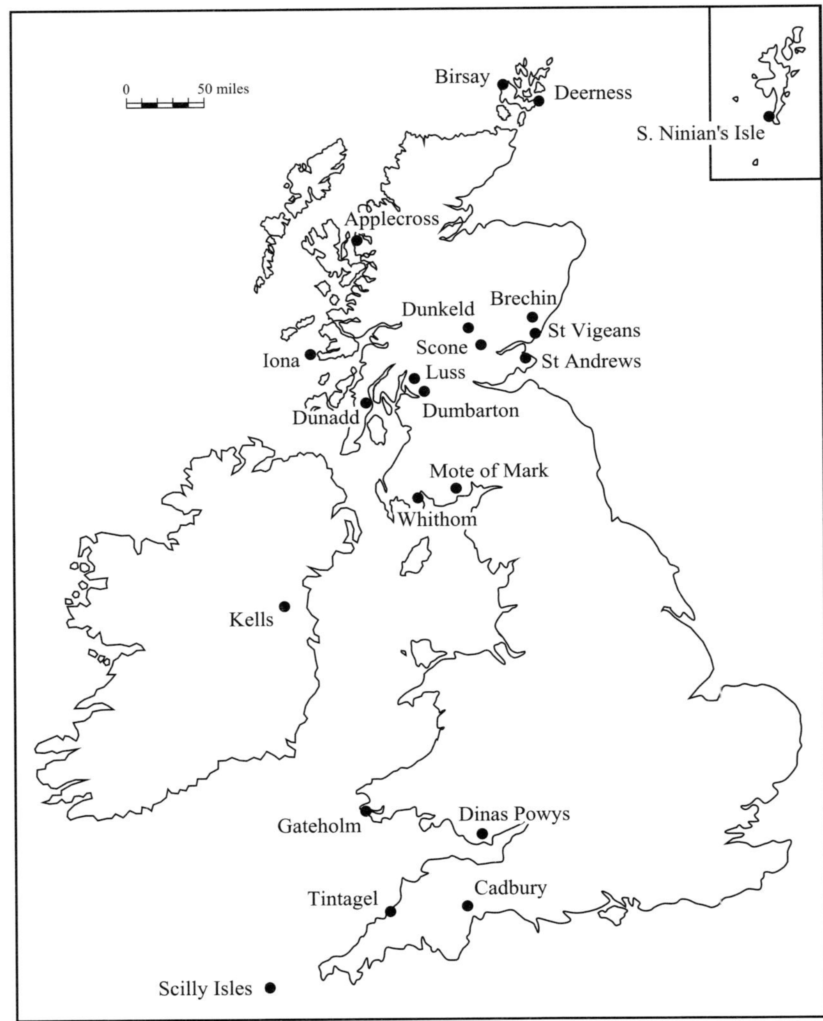

Fig. 1. Places in Dark Age Britain mentioned in the text

Chapter 1

The second Day Conference on Scotland in the Dark Ages was held on 18 February 1995, two years on from the first, which looked at Scotland in a European context. This time the focus was more narrowly on the British Isles in an attempt to see Scotland as part of Celtic Britain-although there was a regrettable absence of input from Ireland. As previously it was intended to make the tone of the Conference inter-disciplinary, and the mix of papers once more provided a stimulating array of different and diverse approaches. Such a recipe certainly seems to provide an acceptable and attractive programme for students and teachers from varying departments, as well as for members of the general public: all of whom are well able to listen to and learn from the presentation of very different research topics by historians, archaeologists, linguists and onomasticians. Once more the numbers prepared to travel to St. Andrews for such an occasion in the middle of winter surprised and delighted the organisers.

Some of our speakers also travelled a fair distance and we were exceedingly grateful to them for being prepared to down tools in the middle of a teaching term and devote time and energy to presenting papers and participating in the event. They are the reason for the success of these occasions which will be clear from the publication of their papers in this volume. All of them produced their disks promptly and helped to make my job as editor that much easier. The value of the day's proceedings is too precious for the spoken word not to reach a wider audience. However unique an experience it is to hear the masters and mistresses of their subject expound in person there is a duty to catch the gems and fix them in precious metal (the printed word!) for their worth to be fully appreciated.

The papers are printed in the order in which they were delivered. Wendy Davies started the proceedings off with a very wide-ranging look at the idea of 'protected space' and the concomitant practice of ecclesiastical sanctuary in early medieval societies. This opened up the various concepts which are evident in Scotland from the Germanic 'girths' to the 'comraich' of Gaelic society (as well as other terms). These can only be understood in the context of the practices of the early medieval church elsewhere. From concepts we moved to visual reality with Elisabeth Okasha's study of the carved and inscribed stones of south-west Britain. She usefully drew comparisons between these and the inscriptions of Pictland, and pointed out that the evidence might suggest a rather higher level of literacy in Pictland than in the south-west.

The next two speakers made the archaeological contribution to the day's events; Christopher Morris brought the situation of 'Dark Age' power centres into focus and presented his case for seeing Birsay in Orkney and Tintagel in the west country as secular residences rather than monastic retreats. Despite his opening comments on the unsuitability of the term 'Dark Age' for the centuries of the post-Roman era it serves a function for me in encapsulating the problems of the period with which this volume and its predecessor are concerned. This is a period in which historical sources are fragmentary, terse and difficult to link into any coherent political narrative; for which reason those of us who are historians need to look to the discipline of archaeology, to place-name studies and to sculptural analysis for illumination.

Ewan Campbell amplified the role of such power centres in Dark Age society by presenting the material evidence for wider contacts and by pointing out the different explanations which can be postulated about trade in such societies. The next two papers presented evidence about the ecclesiastical situation; Simon Taylor shows how place-names can be used to attempt to fill out the thin record of the church's development in eastern Scotland. Thomas Clancy helps us to understand the important place which the Céli Dé reformers had in Scotland in the ninth and tenth centuries by demonstrating the close link between Iona and the Céli Dé reformers in Ireland, and the role of one of the abbots in transmitting the new reforming ideas eastwards to the heartland of the Scotto-Pictish kingdom.

Finally Patrick Wormald ranged magisterially over the whole world of European 'Dark Age' hegemonies while exploring the remarkable change of political power structures in eastern Scotland which is one of the central mysteries of this period. He sees this as a possible example of the violent take-over of power which is manifested elsewhere in Celtic Britain and Germanic Europe, and he puts forward another angle on the Viking role in these turbulent events of the ninth century.

I believe the world of scholarship is enlightened by this collection of diverse studies which I am proud to present to the reading public, and hope that it will help to foster a better understanding of the culture and identity of this country. My thanks are due to the many supporters who have helped me to realise these gatherings; the Committee for Dark-Age Studies in the University of St. Andrews and the Early Medieval Research Group in Edinburgh (EMERGE) in

particular. Professor John Guy, Chairman of the School of History and International Relations in the University provided a warm welcome and alcoholic cheer at lunchtime (which was much appreciated) as well as financial contributions towards Speakers' expenses, as also did the Russell Trust. Graeme Whittington provided the entree to the Dept. of Geography again as well as much practical help on the day. Dr. Ronald Cant as always was generous with moral and financial support in the realization of my Dark Age Studies initiative and the second of the ensuing Conference publications.

Dept. of Medieval History
University of St. Andrews

'Protected Space' in Britain and Ireland in the Middle Ages

Wendy Davies

This is a discursive and speculative paper, intentionally so, since I aim to ring bells in your heads and encourage you to think about possibilities. It does, however, take its starting point from a detailed analysis that I have discussed elsewhere (Davies 1995).[1]

The notion that some clearly defined spaces are places of protection, places where people can be safe, is a familiar one. It is probably best exemplified by the Christian idea of sanctuary (still invoked, for example, by illegal immigrants to Britain) but it is in no way confined to Christian contexts: there are the ancient Greek sanctuaries associated with Diana at Ephesus or Minerva at Sparta, for example, and there are the Levitical cities of refuge of the Old Testament (Timbal Duclaux de Martin 1939: 18-19), while the idea remains common in children's play; even the despised Violet Elizabeth had to be protected by William Brown and his friends when she 'took sanctuary' with them.

In this paper I want to draw your attention to the act of protecting as well as to the places where people could feel protected, although - as we shall see - the two came together in the later middle ages. My comments will relate to Britain and Ireland, and largely to the central middle ages, but I will make some reference to later periods.

Protection

The idea that an individual can legitimately afford protection to another was a norm in early medieval European societies, continental as well as insular. By 'legitimately' I mean that it was a power, and a right, acknowledged by the society surrounding the individual and in several cases articulated in legal collections; Anglo-Saxon law codes offer a good insular example. It was usual for a man's power to protect to be related to his status: the higher his status, the greater that power. This finds its most concrete expression in the graded penalties for breach or violation of protection that feature in many early medieval legal texts: if you killed a man in a bishop's house, the penalty was greater than if you killed him in a priest's house; the offence to the bishop was greater, because his status was higher; and you owed compensation to the bishop for violating his protection in addition to the compensation you owed for the deed itself to the dead man's kin or lord.

So much is standard; it is familiar and well-known. Before going further, I will take a few minutes to consider words for 'protection' and their semantic ranges, since they are important for our understanding of early medieval approaches. In Germanic languages the word for protection is *mund* and in Celtic languages there are words related to the root *snād-*, words like modern Welsh *nawdd*, Old Irish *snádud*, Old Breton *nodet*. The meaning at the core of *mund* is 'hand', and hence its secondary sense of 'protection', taking into the hands of someone. At the core of *snād-* seems to be the meaning 'to bind', and hence its sense of being attached to someone. Both groups of words were used to express the reciprocities that underlie the power and responsibility of the head of a household in the early middle ages: he protects and guards the members of the household, and so they are in his hands and are thereby bound to him; they are in his power; as protector, he receives compensation for offences committed against them. The seventh- and eighth-century Lombard law on *mundium* (the sphere of someone's protection) is prominent: for example, a widow may return to the *mundium* of her near relatives, from that of her husband's relatives, in certain circumstances, and a girl can return to the *mundium* of her relatives if he who holds her *mundium* attacks her (Fischer Drew 1973: 79-80, 85-92, for example). Even in England in the early seventh century, the consequences of infringing protection were explicitly set out in the Laws of Æthelberht, 75 and 76 (Attenborough 1922: 14).

By extension, therefore, the household was a 'safe' place; it was safe because it was protected. It was (or should have been) inviolable.[2] Attacks on or in a household struck at the householder's power of protection and therefore struck at the heart of his own honour and identity. 'Household' here was often explicitly both house and the land around it: to early Icelanders safety extended to the land 'within the fence [round the house]' (Gourevitch 1987: 529); and in Irish secular law, the precinct round the dwelling was explicitly included in the inviolable area - *maigen dígona* (Binchy 1941: 83). Valuing the inviolability of the household was not peculiar to the early middle ages: we still think of an Englishman's home as his castle; the 'homestead' is not just the place where you live but it is the place where you are safe (owning, as I do, a garden across which my neighbours have the only available access to their property, I am

often conscious of a deep-seated sense of outrage when strange vehicles encroach; this is not merely proprietary: I feel threatened and fearful, I start to feel unsafe); and in the *genre* of the Western, the 'bad' men are always the ones who attack the 'good' homesteaders. In the classic film of the early '50s, *Shane*, whenever the bad men cross the stream and enter the protected area around the hero's house, the tension mounts -the music changes - we can read the visual signals - we know that the crossing is a threat to the safety of the hero's family.

In the early middle ages, by a different extension, a man might stretch his power of protection to people beyond the homestead. In England, as late as the early tenth century, a secular man could offer protection to a thief for a limited period, for three days if the protector was a thegn, for nine if he was a king (IV Æthelstan 6 (Attenborough 1922: 148, 150)); if violated, the value of his *mundbyrd* was due to the protector for breach of protection. In Ireland a protector could give legal freedom from distraint (*snádud*), a power for which there were elaborate, status-related rules: protection from distraint could last for fifteen days from one sort of noble (*aire ard*) but only for ten days from a lesser noble (*aire tuíseo*), just as the extent of the *maigen dígona* also varied with rank. So intrinsic was the notion of protection to the fabric of Irish society, that these powers still existed in Ireland, and were exercised, in the late sixteenth century (Kelly 1988: 140-1).[3]

On the continent, by yet another early medieval extension, the word *mundbyrd* in Carolingian Francia came to refer to a special royal protection, given by the ruler to some selected individuals and to monasteries, such as Lorsch: the beneficiary was protected from all harm by the king; if he was harmed, then the guilty one was subject to pay a fine. This case involves an extension of the king's personal power of protection, an extension that reinforced his distinctively royal status (Ganshof 1965: 46).

In the early middle ages the power to protect was an aspect of the status of free men. Its application says much more about the power, privilege and independence of the protector than it does about the status or condition of the individual who came within the sphere of his protection. Hence, in our texts breach of protection attracts far more attention than respect for it. It did so because being able to sustain protective power was essential for the public recognition of status and therefore for the maintenance of social and political order in that world.

The territorialization of protection

There are, of course, other types of 'safe place' than the household and the proximity of a protector; such are the meeting places protected by early Kentish law in England, or the safety of the Icelandic *thing*, or the quiet and order of an Irish court (*airecht*) meeting for judicial business - no anger or incitement was allowed. The reasons for these kinds of safety are different from the safety that derives from a protector and they do not primarily arise from a person's status;[4] rather, they are to do with a community's need to meet and conduct its business without fear of attack. Hence, characteristically, weapons had to be put down by those arriving at the meeting, and drawing a weapon when the meeting was in progress was a particularly serious offence. In early English law these concepts are more frequently expressed by the word *frið* than by *mund*, where *frið* is 'peace', 'security', 'freedom from fighting', and secondarily, 'truce', 'agreement'; *friðstow* is therefore the 'peace-place', the refuge or place of safety. The ideas are distinct from the act of protection inherent in the notion of *mund*.

The power to protect was not without limits, and - at least until the tenth century - there was a tendency to express its extent in temporal terms when it stretched beyond the household; hence, we find protection for thirty days, or whatever period was appropriate.[5] What is so interesting in insular areas is the fact that in certain contexts the power to protect became territorialized beyond the homestead: power to protect could be expressed in relation to a defined space. Hence, in Welsh, *nawdd*, 'protection', gave the word *noddfa*, 'place (*ma*) of protection'. And accordingly offences committed in the *noddfa* brought compensation to the protector as well as to the damaged party. This is most explicitly set out in the southern Welsh, late twelfth-century, Cyfnerth Redaction of the laws: the payments due for offences in the *noddfa* (outside the cemetery) were to be split 50:50 between the abbot and 'learned youths' of the church (Pryce 1993: 180). There are tenth- and eleventh-century cases of compensatory payments of this type being made to clerics - in material from the church of Llandaff, from the South East (Davies 1995: 138-40); and there are many twelfth-century references to the use and violation of specific *noddfeydd* (Pryce 1993: 170-3). There are also examples of apparently comparable compensation being paid to churches in Ireland, as to Armagh for 'outrage' in the late tenth century (Ó Corráin 1978: 22). It is usually assumed that the *termonn* lands that surrounded Irish churches and monasteries marked the physical extent of protected space (Hughes 1966: 148-9; Lucas 1967: 203-4), although the *termonn* is more explicitly associated with refuge and with the limits of the 'holy' in the seventh and eighth centuries (Doherty 1985: 56-9). Armagh, Clonmacnoise, Kildare and Scattery Island certainly had locatable *termonn* lands by the ninth century. Hogan (1910) listed 32 *termonn* names for early Ireland - often associated with a saint's name, like *Termonn Brígte* or *Termonn Ciaráin*. Where these names refer to ecclesiastical space, the space may, as Ann Hamlin has suggested, have been marked out by cross-inscribed stones (Hughes and Hamlin 1977: 80-1).

Now, the territorial expression of protection has a very strong ecclesiastical flavour once it gets beyond the limits of the freeman's homestead. The idea of the protective power of the saints is particularly strong in Old Irish material - witness Colman's Hymn invoking John the Baptist as protection (*snádud*), the early poems from Iona invoking Colum Cille as protection (*snádud*) and the developed analogies of the saint as *lorica*, breastplate (Stokes and Strachan 1903: ii.301; cf. Clancy and Márkus 1995: 153-4, 170). Many of the examples of protected space for which we have good recorded evidence, like Llanbadarn Fawr and Llanddewibrefi in 1109, relate to monasteries and churches.[6]

It could be that we should add to these Welsh and Irish cases the further ecclesiastical examples of the so-called 'chartered sanctuaries' of northern and western England -Hexham, Beverley, Durham, Ripon, St Buryan, and Padstow. Beverley, like several others, had graded penalties for the violators of its 1½ miles of protected space in the late middle ages, increasing as they approached the church (Cox 1911: 126-7); Durham and Hexham had similarly graded penalties at least by the late eleventh century - marked out by crosses (Hall 1989: 426-7). St Buryan and Padstow were both noted for their 'privileged' sanctuaries (Olson 1989: 72, 79). These chartered or privileged sanctuaries look like Welsh protected space because they are significantly different from 'ordinary' sanctuary as we find it in English churches. Their special status was known, and remarked upon by late medieval and early modern travellers like Leland, and some northern cases had special powers in relation to unemendable offences (Hall 1989: 433). The extent of their special space tended to be marked out physically, often by crosses (four at Beverley and Hexham, six at Wetherhal (Cox 1911: 128, 155, 175)); the areas were large - 1-2-3 miles in diameter; and penalties for offences within tended to be graded (as they were in Irish canon and Welsh secular law). Given the English legislation which territorialized protection in the tenth and eleventh centuries (see further below), we should perhaps *expect* them to be comparable. It does not follow that they had all the characteristics of the Welsh *noddfa* (in particular we do not know about the range of punishable offences in the crucial period of the tenth and eleventh centuries) but they are sufficiently similar to be considered in the same light; and sufficiently unlike sanctuary as it is commonly found. We should note that the areas around the salthouses in eleventh-century Nantwich and Middlewich were also especially protected: specified offences committed within a league of the two places attracted fines, although there were no penalties beyond the league (*Cheshire Domesday*, S2 (i.268r)). The latter material, which happens not to be ecclesiastical, provides us with clear evidence that protection was territorialized in practice, and not just in theory, in eleventh-century England.

We should also think of the girths of Scotland, like that mentioned at Luss in 1315 (*RRS* 5: no. 55); Lesmahagow, Innerleithen, Tynninghame and Wedale church (Stow) all have much earlier references, although these earlier, twelfth-century, references use Latin words for the girth (Lawrie 1905: no. 172, *RRS* 1: no.219, *RRS* 2: no.68).[7] 'Girth' is a metathesized form of the late Old English word *griđ*, where *griđ* is a borrowing from Scandinavian *griđ*, whose early semantic range (though not root) was very close to that of *mund*: it had a primary meaning of 'home', 'abode', extended to 'peace', 'truce', 'pardon', and so on; it often meant 'safe conduct' in Old Icelandic (Sørensen 1993: 159). By the eleventh century it could mean in English both 'protection' and also a specific 'peace' or 'truce', limited in space or time. *The Oxford English Dictionary* (*s.v.* grith) cites these meanings of peace and protection but also cites the use of girth for 'place of protection' (both general and specific) from 1300 until the nineteenth century. A high proportion of *OED* citations of this latter usage are in Scottish contexts. Not only do we find 'girth' as the word for ecclesiastically protected areas in Scotland; we also find grithcrosses at Tynemouth; and grithmen attached to northern English church areas, such as Ripon, in the later middle ages (the grithmen may or may not have sought protection - in Scandinavia grithmen were members of the household, whether permanent family members or servants on short-term contracts (Sørensen 1993: 159)). Just as Beverley and Tynemouth had crosses to mark the limits of the protected area, so Lesmahagow had four such crosses by 1144 (Lawrie 1905: 136) and the monastery of Applecross in western Scotland had stone markers to lay out its protected territory - a place to this day known as a'Chomraich in Gaelic, the 'protected place' (MacDonald 1985: 179).[8]

As Professor Barrow pointed out at the conference, it may also be the case that Scottish placenames in *tearmann* - as in Tillytarmont and Drummietermont - point to Gaelic versions of the same phenomenon, given this use of the Irish word *termonn*; hence Clach an Tearmainn, the *termonn* stone, marking the limits of Oronsay Priory in the strand separating Colonsay and Oronsay (Watson 1926: 259). I am not confident, however, that all *termonn* names denoted 'protected' space in the sense used here, particularly in the earliest Christian centuries.[9]

Sanctuary

Whatever its origin, the spatial dimension of extended protection looks largely, though not entirely, ecclesiastical; it is both a reflection of, and a contributor to, the status of specific churches.

By the eleventh century space protected by ecclesiastical bodies in Britain and Ireland also looked like 'sanctuary'; and in part it was. But, it involved a lot more than sanctuary and the reasons for its existence were quite different. Firstly, the physical scale of insular protected space was altogether different from the 'ordinary' sanctuaries we find in Britain and from sanctuary on the continent. In the case of protected space, we are dealing with zones that could be as big as one, two or three miles in radius in Wales, Scotland, and England, as also in some Breton cases: St Asaph reputedly had a mile square (Pryce 1993: 171n); Applecross was twelve miles across (Watson 1926: 125) and Luss three miles 'around' (*RRS* 5: no. 55); Hexham and Ripon were two miles across, Beverley three miles, and St Buryan and Padstow perhaps the same (Cox 1911: 215, 223); and the original *minihi* of Gouesnou in western Brittany was about 1.3 square miles, though later doubled (Tanguy 1984: 15). This contrasts with the classic 30-35-40 metres (*passus*) of sanctuary land around churches on the continent and with the tiny '*sauvetés*' of southern France.[10] Secondly, the nature and scale of the consequences of violation of protected space were altogether different: if an offence was committed in a protected space (theft, abduction, arson, assault, homicide), then it occasioned significant financial compensation to the protector (as well as to the damaged), a compensation supported by secular law, as befitted an issue of personal status. Violation of sanctuary might well require penance, in recognition of the affront to the church, but that was essentially a spiritual matter and did not have to have

material consequences; hence, excommunication was a common penalty for breach of sanctuary. Although the canonists began to discuss the application of secular penalties for breach of sanctuary in the eleventh century, Timbal Duclaux de Martin knew of no actual cases of secular penalties being applied at that time (1939: 207-8; 185, 237).[11]

This difference is hardly surprising given that sanctuary is in essence to do with asylum - refuge. It is a mechanism for ensuring the safety of life and limb for fugitives: at its heart is the legal and social position of the person seeking protection, not the status of the protector. From at least the time of the *Theodosian Code*, churches had provided a place of asylum for fugitive slaves and others (as the Levitical cities of refuge had provided asylum for homicides (Numbers 35)) (Timbal Duclaux de Martin 1939: 83-4). These ideas were quite clearly taken into Irish ecclesiastical thinking by the eighth century, for canons explicitly refer to Old Testament cities of refuge (*Hibernensis* XXVIII; cf. Doherty 1985: 57); as they also reached England by the late seventh century (Laws of Ine 5, Attenborough 1922: 38). Refuge for criminals could certainly be subject to restrictions: there were early medieval distinctions between the refuge rights of accused and condemned criminals. Nevertheless, sanctuary was essentially for fugitives, although ultimately the type of fugitive who could expect to be protected came to be severely limited (thieves and brigands were excluded in the thirteenth century and fifteenth-century papal bulls exempted further categories of offender).

The restrictions of the later middle ages followed an extension of the scope of local sanctuaries on the continent in the years round about AD 1000, in the context of the Peace of God movement: there should be a special peace for a church and the houses around it, like the Catalan precincts known as *sagreres*, sacred places (Head and Landes 1992; Martí 1988). What this meant in practice was a right to freedom from molestation for church property and often, given the prevailing political context, for the poor and defenceless or unarmed. In other words, it meant extending the right of asylum from fugitive criminals to the poor. The movement was taken to extreme lengths in some parts: in north-west Herefordshire (Leominster and neighbourhood) 'refuge cemeteries' were consecrated in the mid twelfth century, which had no associated rights of burial at all; these were places 'for the refuge of the poor in time of hostility' - a sacred refuge without an associated holy focus (Kemp 1988: 86, 89); at the same period Bishop Stephen of Rennes blessed a cemetery 'for the refuge of the

living, not the burial of the dead' in the parish of Marmoutiers (Timbal Duclaux de Martin 1939: 230). Although, therefore, sanctuary was often expanded in western Europe in the eleventh and twelfth centuries, it was not expanded to become protected space after the sense of *nawdd* or *mund*. The idea of asylum remained central.

The chronology of territorialization

This spatial expression of protection does not look especially ancient. I doubt that it started much before the tenth century in Britain. Although the *Hibernensis* and other seventh-/eighth-century Irish texts go to some length to discuss marking out the bounds of holy places (XLIV), by the sign of the cross, they are more concerned with refuge (canonical sanctuary) than with protection (Lucas 1967: 184; Doherty 1985: 56-7).[12]

My preference for the relatively late development of protected space arises for the following reasons. Firstly, it is extremely difficult to find strong and well-evidenced suggestions of the practice before about 900. Secondly, there is a coalescence of English cases of 'chartered sanctuary' attributed to the period of Æthelstan: rightly or wrongly people tended to believe that it was Æthelstan who had confirmed or established the areas. Thirdly, the English legislation on *mund* became noticeably more territorial during the tenth century, and by the time of Æthelred and Cnut was strongly so: Alfred's stress on *periods* of protection gave way to Æthelred's stress on the violation of protected *space* (VIII Æth. 1, 4) (cf. Hall 1989: 431); all churches were in the protection (*griđ*) of God and Christ (VIII Æth. 1, I Cnut 2 (Robertson 1925: 116, 154); while the penalties due to churches for violation of their protection varied since, though all had the same sanctity, all did not have the same status (VIII Æth. 5) - an important clause, emphasizing status and differentiating the authority that derives from status from the authority that comes with holiness. Fourthly, none of the Irish cases of compensation for infringement comes till the late tenth century. Fifthly, as I have argued elsewhere, there are special reasons for believing it to be a tenth-century development in Wales (Davies 1995: 163-4). It is also likely that the change to a territorial approach was influenced by the - intrinsically territorial - canonical law of sanctuary. However, it may be as important that the change was a part of a general shift in attitudes to physical space: land became something to be delimited, ridden

around, and physically dominated, rather than a generalized source of sustenance or a distant source of goods to be plundered and vacated; property literally had to be encompassable.[13]

I would also reinforce the chronological point by focussing on the borrowing of *grið* into English. This is a tenth-century borrowing. In tenth- and eleventh-century English royal legislation *grið* was used in parallel to *mund*: this is quite explicit in the Laws of Cnut, where 'mundbreach' in Wessex is 'grithbreach' in the Danelaw (although the usages are not always so regionally distinctive) (II Cnut 12, 15; Robertson 1925: 180). In fact, by the year 1000 *ciricgrith* was a more common term than *mund* for the protection afforded by the church, whatever the region - and a more common term than the *frið*, peace, of the church, though the terminology is not stable (by the eleventh and twelfth centuries Latin *pax* could refer both to a specifically given protection and to a general peace). It looks as if English ideas began to change round about 900: it has been argued that the Laws of Alfred started to equate church peace with house protection (Riggs 1963: 34); and in Edward and Guthrum's Peace (2.1) *ciricgrið* was to be as inviolate as the specific protection given by the king (the king's *handgrið*). The earlier 'peace' (*frið*) was becoming the 'protected area'; the protected area was more than a refuge for criminals (ie more than sanctuary): penalties for violation of the ecclesiastical protected area in the tenth and eleventh centuries could be heavy; and perhaps some special protected areas, of considerable size, were marked out on the ground.

****

We have come a long way from the simple sphere of a freeman's protection, his 'home'. Quite different ideas like canonical sanctuary (the consecrated refuge) came to Britain and Ireland and influenced approaches to church territory; moreover, approaches to protected space continued to change and develop. In England, Scotland and Wales, over time, the protected space could become an immunity (an area exempt from the demands of others, such as demands for taxes or to inspect) or could even become a *seigneurie* (an area which a lord set out to dominate, over which he pro-actively established control, by exercising judicial powers and setting up monopolies). This *could* happen to the *noddfa*, though it did not necessarily do so. It is true of Llandaff by the early twelfth century, with its royal exemptions, and its rights to hold courts, market and mint (Davies 1995: 150-2). It is true of Beverley and Ripon by the thirteenth century (and possibly even by the late eleventh century), with their extensive jurisdictional rights and powers (Lobel 1934: 126); it is true of the late medieval *minihi* in Brittany (Chédeville and Tonnerre 1987: 354, 358) and it is true of Luss by the early fourteenth century, with its rights of criminal jurisdiction (*RRS* 5: no. 55). In other words, the protected space so contributed to the status of some particular institutions that it became the core of wider powers; and of the successsful attempts of some lords to turn power over land into power over people.

Protecting space gave considerable financial and practical powers to some major religious bodies in the tenth and eleventh centuries - the period at the heart of the development. We do not need to explain these newly acquired powers in terms of the devolution and fragmentation of royal or imperial power (as historians are prone to do for the continent). Indeed, in some insular cases new ecclesiastical powers seemed to develop as a response to increasing rather than decreasing ruler power: in Wales it was a defensive reaction against ruler aggression; in England the church's power to protect became in part an expression of ruler power, for each reinforced the other.

****

It was my purpose in giving this talk to draw attention to protecting space in Britain and Ireland and stimulate some further thought. The phenomenon is a commonplace for historians of early medieval Ireland and Wales. It looks as if it may be as characteristic of England in the tenth and eleventh centuries, particularly in view of the framing of English legislation and the evidence of *Domesday Book*; and perhaps it may not be quite so characteristic of Ireland as is commonly assumed - at least at the early, seventh- and eighth-century, period. The same does not appear to be true of the continent, with its much greater emphases on ecclesiastical immunities. The use that insular ecclesiastical bodies initially made of protected space had some of the same consequences for them as the early immunity had for Frankish churches - additional income (Fouracre 1995); in political terms it was the functional equivalent of the Frankish immunity.

What is significant about this institution is not the mere delimitation of a special space but the distinctive nature of the powers exercised within the

space. It is these that differentiate protection from sanctuary. The subject could tolerate a much lengthier investigation, particularly with reference to what happened inside the English chartered sanctuaries, but also with reference to continental similarities and divergences; and indeed with some detailed attention to the Scottish and Irish *termonn* - the word itself has a quite different range of reference from Welsh *noddfa* (borrowed from Latin *terminus*, boundary) and we should perhaps be looking at *comrach* rather than *termonn* for close parallels. I hope others will pursue the trail: not only does it look rich; but it lies at the heart of strategies for establishing and sustaining power, both personal and corporate. And that is central to our understanding of social and political development in the early middle ages.[14]

Appendix

A note on ecclesiastical immunities

By the tenth century the continental immunity (a privilege which freed the holder of immune lands from various kinds of public intervention in those lands, especially with regard to taxation and public systems of justice) was largely an ecclesiastical phenomenon - one that had points of contact with 'protected space'. If the immunist took fines for offences committed within the immunity, this must have looked rather like the consequences of violation of 'protection'. However, although some control of judicial process might lie in the hands of an ecclesiastical immunist lord, the process still in theory remained public and there is no reason to believe that offences committed in the immunity but outside the sanctuary (eg theft between lay persons) carried *additional* compensations to the ecclesiastical lord over and above the 'public' fine. The pre-twelfth-century immunity is therefore very different from 'protected space'. In any case, at least in the Carolingian period, those guilty of major crimes had to be handed over to public authority by the immunist. And, further, we have reservations nowadays about the power of the immunist even in relation to minor offences (Fouracre 1995: 58-68). By the twelfth century, canonists began to apply penalties for violation of immunity to violation of sanctuary and this made the distinction between sanctuary right and ecclesiastical immunity less clear than it had been before (Timbal Duclaux de Martin 1939: 147-58, 185-96); these are late developments, however, and do not affect the clear distinctions of the seventh to eleventh centuries.

There is another type of immunity, sometimes called the 'narrow immunity' by continental scholars, which also has features which resemble insular protected space. The twelfth-century canonists argued that *every* church had a *special* immunity stretching for 30 (and in some cases 40) paces (*passus*); if anyone committed sacrilege by injuring or stealing from clerics within this area, then they were liable to pay a money fine (Gratian *Decretum*, C.17, q.4, c.21). Although the size of this zone was similar to the 30-40 paces of the sanctuary zone, the offence committed was quite distinct from violation of sanctuary; both were sacrilege, but damaging clerics near the church was a different kind of sacrilege. The special immunity was therefore different from sanctuary right in canonist thinking. This special immunity was also differentiated from 'protected space' by its small size and by the absence of secular enforcement of its provisions; and, in any case, the extent to which the canonists' theory was put into practice is very uncertain (and would repay some examination).

There were, then, two different kinds of immunity in canonist thinking, and each was different from sanctuary. I would argue that all three were different from pre-twelfth-century 'protected space', although the 'ordinary' immunity could be comparable in size and the 'special' immunity could in theory involve payment of fines to a church. The similarities are such that, despite the differences, it seems reasonable to propose that the Frankish immunity performed much the same function for continental churches as protected space did for insular churches; and that by the twelfth and thirteenth centuries protected space could easily become the core of an insular immunity.[15]

University College London
2 July 1995

Abbreviations ~~~~~~

Cáin Adamnáin: ed. K. Meyer, Anecdota Oxoniensia, Medieval and Modern Series 12, Oxford 1905.

Le Cartulaire de Redon: ed. A. de Courson, Paris 1863.

Cheshire Domesday: *Domesday Book*, vol. 26, *Cheshire*, ed. P. Morgan (general editor J. Morris), Chichester 1978.

Decretum Magistri Gratiani: in *Corpus Iuris Canonici*, ed. E. Friedberg, 2 vols., Leipzig 1879-81.

Hibernensis: *Die irische Kanonensammlung*, ed. H. Wasserschleben, 2nd edn Leipzig 1885.

RRS 1: *Regesta Regum Scottorum*, vol. 1, *The Acts of Malcolm IV King of Scots 1153-65*, ed. G. W. S. Barrow, Edinburgh 1960.

RRS 2: *Regesta Regum Scottorum*, vol. 2, *The Acts of William I King of Scots 1165-1214*, ed. G. W. S. Barrow, Edinburgh 1971.

RRS 5: *Regesta Regum Scottorum*, vol. 5, *The Acts of Robert I King of Scots 1306-29*, ed. A. A. M. Duncan, Edinburgh 1988.

References ~~~~~~

Attenborough, F. L. (ed. and trans.) 1922, *The Laws of the Earliest English Kings*, Cambridge.

Binchy, D. A. (ed.) 1941, *Críth Gablach*, Dublin.

Chédeville, A. and Tonnerre, N.-Y. 1987, *La Bretagne féodale XI*^{e}-*XIII*^{e} *siècle*, Rennes.

Clancy, T. O. and Márkus, G. 1995, *Iona. The Earliest Poetry of a Celtic Monastery*, Edinburgh.

Cox, J. C. 1911, *The Sanctuaries and Sanctuary Seekers of Medieval England*, London.

Davies, W. 1995, 'Adding Insult to Injury: Power, Property and Immunities in Early Medieval Wales' in W. Davies and P. Fouracre (eds.), *Property and Power in the Early Middle Ages*, Cambridge, pp. 137-64.

Davies, W. and Fouracre, P. (eds.) 1995, *Property and Power in the Early Middle Ages*, Cambridge.

Doherty, C. 1985, 'The monastic town in early medieval Ireland' in H. B. Clarke and A. Simms (eds.), *The Comparative History of Urban Origins in Non-Roman Europe*, British Archaeological Reports International Series 255(i), pp. 45-75.

Edwards, N. 1990, *The Archaeology of Early Medieval Ireland*, London.

Fischer Drew, K. (trans.) 1973, *The Lombard Laws*, Philadelphia.

Fouracre. P. 1995, 'Eternal light and earthly needs: practical aspects of the development of Frankish immunities' in W. Davies and P. Fouracre (eds.), *Property and Power in the Early Middle Ages*, Cambridge, pp. 53-81.

Ganshof, F. L. 1965, *Frankish Institutions under Charlemagne*, trans. B. and M. Lyon, New York 1968.

Gourevitch, A. J. 1987, 'Semantics of the medieval community: "farmstead", "land", "world" (Scandinavian example)' in *Les communautés rurales*, pt 5, *Recueils de la société Jean Bodin pour l'histoire comparative des institutions* vol. 44, Paris, pp. 525-40.

Hall, D. 1989, 'The Sanctuary of St Cuthbert' in G. Bonner, D. Rollason, C. Stancliffe (eds.), *St Cuthbert, his Cult and his Community to AD 1200*, Woodbridge, pp. 425-36.

Head, T. and Landes, R. (eds.) 1992, *The Peace of God: Social Violence and Religious Response in France around the Year 1000*, Ithaca and London.

Hogan, E. 1910, *Onomasticon Goedelicum Locorum et Tribum Hiberniae et Scotiae*, Dublin.

Hughes, K. 1966, *The Church in Early Irish Society*, London.

Hughes, K. and Hamlin, A. 1977, *The Modern Traveller to the Early Irish Church*, London.

Kelly, F. 1988, *A Guide to Early Irish Law*, Dublin.

Kemp, B. 1988, 'Some aspects of the *parochia* of Leominster in the twelfth century' in J. Blair (ed.), *Minsters and Parish Churches. The Local Church in Transition*, Oxford, pp. 83-95.

Lawrie, A. C. 1905, *Early Scottish Charters*, Glasgow.

Le Moing, J.-Y. 1988, 'Toponymie bretonne de Haute-Bretagne', Thèse de Doctorat, Université de Rennes 2, 2 vols.

Le Moing, J.-Y. 1990, *Les noms de lieux bretons de Haute-Bretagne*, Spezed.

Lobel, M. D. 1934, 'The ecclesiastical banleuca in England' in F. M. Powicke (ed.), *Oxford Essays in Medieval History presented to Herbert Edward Salter*, Oxford, pp. 122-40.

Lucas, A. T. 1967, 'The plundering and burning of churches in Ireland, 7th to 16th century' in E. Rynne (ed.), *North Munster Studies*, Limerick, pp. 172-229.

MacDonald, A. D. S. 1985, 'Iona's style of government among the Picts and Scots: the toponymic evidence of Adomnán's Life of Columba', *Peritia* 4, pp. 174-86.

Martí, R. 1988, 'L'Ensagrerament: l'adveniment de les *sagreres* feudals', *Faventia* 10, pp. 153-82.

Ó Corráin, D. 1978, 'Nationality and kingship in pre-Norman Ireland' in T. W. Moody (ed.), *Nationality and the Pursuit of National Independence*, Belfast, pp. 1-35.

Olson, L. 1989, *Early Monasteries in Cornwall*, Woodbridge.

Pryce, H. 1993, *Native Law and the Church in Medieval Wales*, Oxford.

Riggs, C. H. 1963, *Criminal Asylum in Anglo-Saxon Law*, University of Florida Monographs 18, Gainesville.

Robertson, A. J. 1925, *The Laws of the Kings of England from Edmund to Henry I*, Cambridge.

Sørensen, P. Meulengracht 1993, *Fortælling og ære. Studier i islændingesagaerne*, Aarhus.

Stokes, W. and Strachan, J. (eds.) 1901-3, *Thesaurus Palaeohibernicus*, 2 vols., Cambridge.

Tanguy, B. 1984, 'La troménie de Gouesnou. Contribution à l'histoire des minihis en Bretagne', *Annales de Bretagne*, 91, pp. 9-25.

Timbal Duclaux de Martin, P. 1939, *Le droit d'asile*, Paris.

Watson, W. J. 1926, *The History of the Celtic Place-Names of Scotland*, Edinburgh.

Notes

1 I owe thanks to Professor Richard Bailey, whose comments in a coach on a trip to Luss first stimulated me to think about these issues.

2 Note that even in late eleventh-century Cheshire offences in the homestead - *in domo* - carried a special fine (*Cheshire Domesday*, C4 (i. 262v)).

3 Violation of the legal protection of a freeman by killing or injuring someone under protection was the offence known as *díguin* in Irish law. Binchy (1941: 83) points out that the meaning of *díguin* extended to include 'breach of house-peace', where the 'house-peace' encompassed the surrounding precinct as well as the house.

4 Although, if a king presided at a meeting, it would of course reinforce the safe status of the occasion.

5 In Ireland, at least, the limits also included certain types of person; some could never be protected - a runaway slave, a runaway wife, a killer, a son who failed to look after his father; this clearly distinguishes the rules about protection from those about sanctuary (Kelly 1988: 141).

6 Breton *minihi* (< Latin *monachia*, monastic land) may have been used in a fashion similar to *noddfa*, although its usages were clearly various (Chédeville and Tonnerre 1987: 354-8). The vernacular term was in use already in the mid-ninth century (*Cartulaire de Redon* nos. 141, 142, 181, 193), although it is not clear that it had any meaning at that period beyond 'monastic land' - some of which was already in lay hands. From the later middle ages the term meant sanctuary, in the conventional sense (Tanguy 1984: 24). The place-name *minihi* tends to occur in western Brittany and also in the North East (Le Moing 1988: ii.78; Le Moing 1990: 234; Tanguy 1984). Most frequently of parish size (eg Gouesnou, Locronan), a few *minihi* were enormous (more than eleven parishes round Tréguier) and some were very much smaller than the parish (eg Gouézec); they were sometimes marked out by crosses. Given the parish size of the majority, it is worth considering the possibility that the *minihi* took on the meaning of ecclesiastical protected space in the tenth and eleventh centuries; the Life of St Goulven emphasizes the inviolability of the saint's space at Goulven, Finistère (Tanguy 1984: 21-2).

7 I am extremely grateful to Professor Geoffrey Barrow for supplying me with references to girths and *tearmann* names after the February conference.

8 For the anglicized Irish word *comrick*, 'legal protection', which was used in English official documents in Ireland in the late middle ages and early modern period, see Kelly 1988: 141n; also Binchy 1941: 107, on different Irish words for 'protection'. (Irish *commairce*, and other words for protection, seem to have replaced *snádud* in the later middle ages.)

9 It is also unlikely that monastic *valla*, earthworks delimiting an area around a monastery, as identified in Ireland, were to delimit 'protected space': they define much smaller areas than the protected spaces we know about (Edwards 1990: 106-12).

10 However, unusually, St Denis claimed a large area (Timbal Duclaux de Martin 1939: 160).

11 Of course, continental ecclesiastical immunities may have *looked like* 'protected space' in the insular sense in the tenth and eleventh centuries, but they were different in their operation (Davies and Fouracre 1995: 12-16, 256-8); see further, Appendix.

12 There is a germ of the protective notion in *Hibernensis* XLIV.8, with its warnings against the violation of holy places by homicide and theft, but the starting point is different - pollution of the holy -and at this stage the penalties appear to be purely ecclesiastical (ie penance). There is another germ of comparability in that penances were graded in accordance with the status of the sanctuary as well as the nature of the offence - a recognition of the importance of status (cf. Doherty 1985: 57-8). Within another couple of centuries some churches were claiming a right to secular penalties (*díre*) - not just penance - for offences committed by laymen within the *termonn*, enforced by secular rulers (*Cáin Adamnáin*, 36). Though the conceptual approach is different here, the application of such claims must have had effects which were indistinguishable from the effects of violation of protected space; in other words, when such claims came to be acknowledged, the *termonn* became like the *noddfa*.

13 There were strong feelings at the conference that the Irish and western Scottish development must have been earlier. The Irish development could of course have been precocious; but the signs are that (i) the Irish *termonn* in the seventh and eighth centuries essentially marked out a place of refuge, safety and safe-keeping, as it continued to do in the central and later middle ages (Lucas 1967); (ii) some of the *termonn* lands took on the attributes of a protected area in the ninth/tenth centuries (see also above, n. 12). Apart from the claims of seventh-century Armagh to an unbelievably large area within its *terminus*, we have little idea of the size of the *termonn* in the early middle ages. All this would benefit from a much closer and more systematic examination - and a closer look at what happened inside a *termonn*.

14 I understand that Dr Brian Golding, of the University of Southampton, is currently working on a book on English sanctuary; this will be a very welcome addition to the existing literature.

15 I am very grateful to my colleague David d'Avray for assistance with canonist texts.

The Early Christian Carved and Inscribed Stones of south-west Britain

Elisabeth Okasha

In this paper the early Christian stones of south-west Britain are described and illustrated and some comparisons are then made with the Pictish inscriptions of Scotland. The texts of the inscriptions discussed and the system of transliteration employed are given in the Appendix. For a full discussion of the south-western stones see Okasha 1993 and of the Pictish (non-ogham) stones see Okasha 1985. Five of the inscriptions discussed are illustrated in the accompanying figures and illustrations of all appear in one or more of Allen and Anderson 1903, Okasha 1985 and Okasha 1993.

The term 'south-west Britain' is used to refer to the south-west peninsula of England, that is, to the counties of Cornwall and Devon. This term, rather than for example 'south-west England', is used since the Cornish (though not those from Devon) regard themselves with some historical justification as Celtic not English. In part of the Romano-British and early Christian periods, in the fourth, fifth and sixth centuries AD, this area did indeed comprise the Celtic kingdom of Dumnonia. Exact details of the fate of Dumnonia are sketchy, but the general drift is clear: from the seventh century onwards the Anglo-Saxons fought their way into Dumnonia and pushed the Celts further south and west. By the late tenth century the whole area was under some sort of Anglo-Saxon control.

In the context of carved and inscribed stones, the term 'early Christian' is used to refer to the entire period from the withdrawal of the Roman legions from Britain up to the Norman Conquest, in round figures from AD 400 to AD 1100. 'Early Christian' is thus a term of chronology and does not imply that all the stones were erected by or for Christians. Some of them certainly were, those which consist of or contain a cross, for example, or those including a Christian symbol like the *chi-rho*. Some of the rest probably were, but we cannot be sure.

There are 69 inscribed stones from this period still in existence and a further ten, though now lost, are known to have existed in modern times. This number may gradually rise. There is, for example, a newly found stone from Kenidjack near St Just in Penwith which contains a letter S followed by two letters, possibly an F and a C. Charles Thomas has recently suggested that this is a genuine new inscription (Thomas 1994, 289). It may be that caution is required here; the inscribing looks rather too deep and fresh to be early Christian and the text may be better considered as later graffiti, perhaps someone's initials. However the general point remains valid that new inscriptions and new pieces of sculpture are likely to turn up in the course of archaeological and other investigation.

Most of the 79 inscribed stones fall into one of three categories: crosses, altar slabs or pillar-stones. The crosses are of course Christian monuments and there are hundreds of crosses in Cornwall dating from the ninth to the eleventh centuries, although most of them are not inscribed. Absolute figures are hard to give. At present there is being undertaken a pilot survey of all the pre-Conquest sculptured stones of the ancient hundred of Penwith. In Penwith there are 25 sculptured stones which are reasonably certain to date from the pre-Conquest period. A cross from Sancreed, for example, (Fig. 2.1) contains a crucifixion figure with a halo, set inside a beaded cross-head; beneath are panels of interlace, now rather worn, and an inscription. The right hand side contains a serpentine creature and the left hand side has diagonal key pattern. On the back there is interlace on both the head and the shaft. The interlace carving suggests that the cross can be dated to the tenth or eleventh centuries.

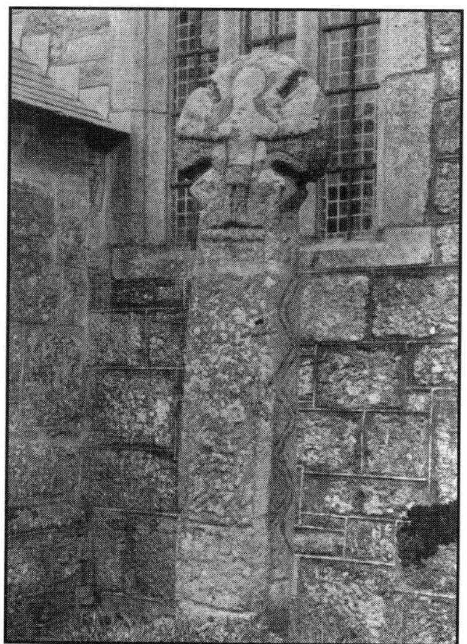

Fig. 2.1 Cross from Sancreed, Cornwall (photograph Royal Commission on Historical Monuments of England)

Much less easy to date are those crosses that contain only a crucifixion figure and no other ornament. There are 28 such crosses in Penwith. Some of these crosses may belong to the early Christian period, but it is hard, in the absence of ornament, to decide which ones are early and how long the tradition of erecting them continued.

Then there are at least 100 uncarved, uninscribed crosses and cross-bases in the area. It is virtually impossible to put a date on crosses of this sort. Some may date from before the Norman Conquest, others may date from the early medieval period, some might even be from modern times.

The preliminary figures for Penwith are: 25 stones with pre-Conquest ornament, 28 with crucifixion figures only, and around 100 with no carving. If Penwith is typical of south-west Britain, or even just of Cornwall, we are clearly talking of hundreds of pre-Conquest monuments, but of how many hundreds is not altogether clear.

Only eleven of the actual crosses are inscribed although there are also three cross-bases that may have had inscriptions and there are three inscribed stones which were subsequently re-cut to form crosses. The inscribed crosses usually have the text integrated into the design of the carving, often in a panel of its own. The texts usually read horizontally and the lettering is most often in a predominantly insular, as opposed to a predominantly capital, script. The cross from Lanherne in Cornwall (Fig. 2.2) is one of the best-preserved of the inscribed crosses and it exhibits all these features. The text on one side reads RŪHOL, presumably a personal name RUNHOL, a name that is likely to be Celtic. Runhol may have carved the cross or have commissioned it to be carved. The text on the other side is quite legible but is hard to interpret. It reads BREID [ET] [I]MAH and may consist of two personal names joined by ET, though this conclusion is based on little but the well-known epigraphic principle that if something is incomprehensible it must be a personal name. If these are personal names their etymology is uncertain.

Fig. 2.2 Cross from Lanherne, Cornwall (photograph Woolf/Greenham Collection)

As well as eleven inscribed crosses, there are two inscribed altar slabs. The one from Camborne in Cornwall is in use as a side altar in the south aisle of the parish church of St Martin and St Meriadoc. Its text reads LEUIUT IUSIT HEC ALTARE PRO ANIMA SUA, 'Leuiut ordered this altar for his own soul'. The Latin is irregular in spelling, grammar and syntax: IUSIT for *iussit* is followed not by an infinitive but by a direct object HEC ALTARE. The classical *altaria* (neuter plural) occurs, as is common in medieval Latin, as ALTARE and so HEC is presumably neuter and accusative, though whether it represents *hoc* (singular) or *haec* (plural) is unclear. The altar slab is dated to the tenth or eleventh centuries on the evidence of its T-fret carving. LEUIUT is probably a Celtic name, though it could possibly be English; there is for example a name *leuiet* in Domesday Book which has been explained as a spelling of the Old English name *leofgeat.*

These crosses and altar slabs, containing interlace and other designs, may be crude by the standards of contemporary sculpture from these islands. They do, however, represent at least an attempt to produce works of art and some of them are aesthetically pleasing. They are also indubitably Christian and they can be dated within reasonable limits, probably from the ninth to the eleventh or twelfth centuries. When we turn to the third category of inscribed stones, the memorial stones known as pillar-stones, the position is rather different. Firstly, there are many more inscribed pillar-stones than there are inscribed crosses or altar slabs; there are 51, of which two are now lost. Secondly, they are typically pieces of uncarved granite which often seem to have been left in the crude shape in which they were picked up from an outcrop of rock. Sometimes, however, they have been rudely shaped into pillars and sometimes the inscribed surfaces have been roughly dressed. Thirdly, many of them lack any specific indication of Christianity. Fourthly, they are difficult to date with any precision and some can only be dated within the broad limits of the fifth or sixth to the eleventh century.

The stone from Welltown near Cardinham in Cornwall is a typical pillar-stone (Fig. 2.3). The text is set without any margins or panels and reads vertically downwards with the bottoms of the letters to the viewer's left. The text reads [VA]ILAT[H]I [F]ILI VROCH[ANI], probably to be interpreted '(the stone) of [Va]ilat[h]us, son of Vroch[anus]'. This formula is frequently encountered. The names are Celtic, probably specifically Irish. The script used is predominantly capital with an occasional insular form. The only carving is the incised arc above the text and there is no explicit sign of Christianity. It is

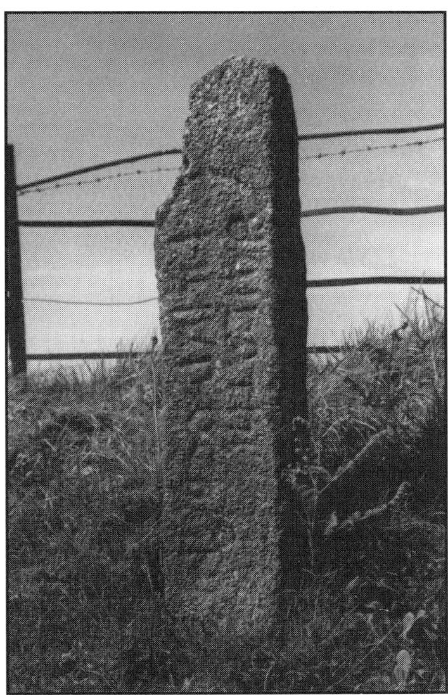

Fig. 2.3 Pillar-stone from Welltown, Cornwall (photograph Woolf/Greenham Collection)

likely to date from the fifth or sixth to the eighth century.

Several of these features can be observed again on the stone from Southill. Like the Welltown stone, this stone is fairly untypical in having a legible text, but it is quite typical in that the text is in a predominantly capital script, is set without panels or margins and reads vertically downwards facing left. The text reads CVMREGNI FILI MAVCI, '(the stone) of Cumregnus, son of Maucus' where the name CVMREGNI is Latin and MAVCI is probably Celtic. Above the text is a double arc and above it a cross, or perhaps a monogram *chi-rho,* indicating that the stone was erected by or for a Christian. This stone exemplifies two common epigraphic features of pillar-stones: the use of the letter I set horizontally and the use of a particular form of the ligature F/I. These features are confined to inscribed stones from the south-west and from Wales, with the one exception of horizontal I used twice on a stone from Santon, Isle of Man (Nash-Williams 1950, 11). The Southill stone probably dates from the sixth to the eighth century.

One other sort of text occurring on the pillar-stones is the Christian formula *hic iacet* 'here lies', often spelt IC IACIT. The use of this formula implies of course that such stones were not just memorial stones but specifically grave-stones. An example occurs on a stone from St Just. The monogram *chi-rho* is incised on one face, neatly set within margins, while on one of the sides is the text SELVS IC IACIT, 'Selus lies here', with the last I horizontal. There are two smaller letters, probably reading NI, above the name SELVS and these may indicate a spelling correction; that is, the name could be either SELVS or

SENILVS, both Latin names, or SELNIVS, which would be more difficult to explain. This stone, like the previous one, is likely to date from the sixth to the eighth century.

A few of the pillar-stones contain texts in both roman and ogham script. The use of ogham script is one of the features which suggests an early date for a stone, from the fifth or sixth century to the eighth century. An example of a stone with ogham is one of the ones from Lewannick in north Cornwall (Fig. 2.4). It has a text in capitals which probably reads [HIC] IACIT VLC[A]GNI, '[here] lies (the body) of Ulc[a]gnus'. The personal name is Irish and occurs also on another stone from south-west Britain, from Nanscow in Cornwall. On the Lewannick stone, the two ogham texts are also both renderings of this same name. Both read from the top down, one on the left hand edge and the other on the right hand edge of the stone. It seems likely that one person was commemorated three times on this stone, rather than that three people with the same name shared one memorial. The Lewannick stone therefore appears to be bi-literal, with part of the text repeated in a different script.

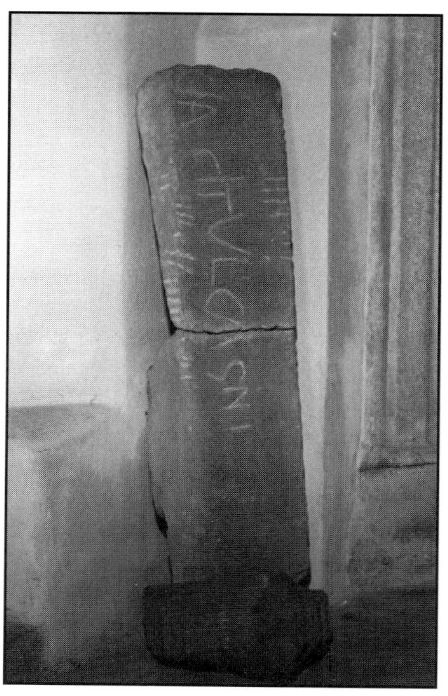

Fig. 2.4 Pillar-stone from Lewannick, Cornwall (photograph Woolf/Greenham Collection)

This is not the case with at least one of the other stones with an ogham text, that from Fardel in Devon, now in the British Museum. This stone is interesting because the language of its texts may be not Latin, as is usually the case, but Irish. It contains four texts, two in capitals and two in ogham. One capital text reads FANONI MAQVIRINI and one ogham text reads MAQIQICI. These texts could be explained as having three Celtic names, the last two specifically Irish; alternatively they could contain the early Irish word MAQVI or MAQI meaning 'son', followed by personal names. The other ogham text reads SAFFAQQUCI, probably a Celtic name. The second capital text probably reads G[A]G[R]A[NV]I, presumably a personal name though of obscure etymology. The Fardel stone thus appears to commemorate several different people and its texts are not bi-literal in the sense that they do not repeat parts of each other in a different script. If some of these texts are in the Irish language then this stone is unique amongst south-western monuments in this respect.

There is one other stone from south-west Britain which is unique on account of its language. This is the stone from Lanteglos in Cornwall which has a text in English. The text is now difficult to read and it has deteriorated since I first examined it in 1964. Using readings made in 1964 and 1985, a text can be reconstructed: AELSEL[Đ] 7 GENE[REĐ] [W]O[H]TE ÞYS[N]E [S]YB[STEL] FOR AELWYNEYS S[O]UL 7 [F]OR HEY[SEL]. The text can be translated 'Aelsel[đ] and Gene[ređ] made this ?family-place (*or* place of peace) for Aelwyn's soul and for ?themselves (*or* Hey[sel])'. The text contains some difficulties but certain things are clear. The language is clearly English (not Latin or a Celtic language) and is late in date, probably eleventh-century at the earliest. Features typical of English of this date are the lack of inflection on S[O]UL, the loss of *r* in the word [W]O[H]TE 'made', and the spellings of the personal names, spellings which can be paralleled in Domesday Book.

It has to be admitted that this stone is rather an embarrassment. Its language clearly proves that it cannot be dated to earlier than the eleventh century. The date-range of the pillar-stones has therefore to be extended to include the eleventh century. If the Lanteglos stone did not exist, one could terminate the series about two centuries earlier. Some people do so: Charles Thomas, for example, dismisses the Lanteglos stone as a 'fossil' (Thomas 1994, 327) and dates the series of pillar-stones to the fifth to the seventh centuries. To ignore the inconvenient is of course one way of dealing with the evidence; another way is to put forward a model that accommodates it. It seems to me that there is no alternative but to admit that pillar-stones were still being erected in the eleventh century. In this context we should note that in Wales there are two Class I stones dating from the eleventh or twelfth centuries, although the rest of this series of stones are dated no later than the ninth century. The two stones are those from Heneglwys and Llangors (Nash-Williams 1950, no. 5, p. 53 and no. 60, p. 76. See also Dark 1992, 60).

The position regarding the early Christian inscribed stones of south-west

Britain can be summarised thus: there are 79 inscribed stones, including ten now lost, ranging in date from the fifth or sixth to the eleventh centuries. These inscribed stones are mainly pillar-stones though some are crosses and other monuments. Roman script, either capital or insular, is used and there are six stones which have in addition an ogham text. The language used is generally Latin although there is one stone which has an English text and one which may have Irish ones. Many texts commemorate individuals and the majority of these people have Celtic names; sometimes we can be more precise and say that the personal names are specifically either Irish or Welsh/Cornish, sometimes we cannot. The non-Celtic names are either English or Latin.

Some useful points of comparison can be made between these stones and the inscriptions from Pictland, that is, that area of Scotland which was under Pictish control during the seventh, eighth and early ninth centuries. Included here are inscriptions from the area in the west which was intermittently under Pictish domination in this period. To facilitate comparison with the stones of south-west Britain, the position is first summarised and then discussed in more detail.

There are some 45 Pictish inscriptions, ranging in date from the seventh to the ninth centuries. The inscriptions on stone occur on a range of monuments, pillar-stones, cross-slabs and, in particular, Class I and II symbol stones; they also occur on objects other than stones, for example the St Ninian's Isle chape and a knife handle from North Uist. Only one script, either roman or ogham, is used on any one stone, except for one rather doubtful stone, from Newton, Aberdeenshire, which might contain both. The languages used are Latin and Pictish and the personal names are Pictish, early Gaelic or Latin.

The first point of comparison that can be drawn concerns the actual number of artifacts. In both areas, the number of inscribed monuments compared to those uninscribed is quite small. However, while the 79 inscribed stones of south-west Britain cover a period of six or seven centuries, the 45 or so Pictish inscriptions cover only two or three centuries. There are, that is, considerably more surviving inscriptions per century from Pictland than from south-west Britain. Of course the number of surviving monuments may reflect not numbers of original monuments so much as things like the subsequent use of the land, the density of population on it during the last millennium, and the amount of archaeological investigation that has taken place there in the last century. However, these three factors, later land-use, population density and quantity of archaeological investigation, are probably broadly similar between the two areas under discussion. This would not be the case if, for example, either area were compared to Anglo-Saxon England.

The numbers of surviving monuments suggest that literacy was more widespread in Pictland than in south-west Britain. Another piece of evidence suggesting the same thing is the wide range of Pictish monuments and artifacts containing inscriptions. In the south-west, inscriptions occur mainly on unsculptured pillar-stones with a few on other stone monuments like decorated crosses and altar slabs. In Pictland there are inscriptions on various sorts of stones and also on other objects. The ninth-century stone from St Vigeans, for example, is a cross-slab. It has interlace carving above the text and further carving on all sides, including Pictish symbols on the back. The text is a memorial one and probably reads DROSTEN IRE UORET [E]TT FORCUS. It contains three personal names, the first two being Pictish and the third Gaelic. The names are joined by [E]TT, presumably Latin *et*, and by IRE (or possibly IPE). A recent article by Thomas Clancy makes the neat and convincing suggestion that IRE could be interpreted as *i ré,* Old Irish/Gaelic for 'in the reign of' (Clancy 1993, 345-53). As Clancy points out, mixed Gaelic/Latin inscriptions are known from Ireland although admittedly *i ré* is not elsewhere recorded in any inscription.

Another ninth-century inscribed cross-slab, that from Brechin, has no abstract sculpture or symbols but a complex set of Christian figure carving. The text, with its abbreviations expanded, reads SANCTA MARIA MATER CHRISTI, 'St Mary, mother of Christ'. This is not a memorial text but a descriptive one, describing the central carved figure. An example of an inscription on a Class 1 symbol stone is that from Brandsbutt, Inverurie, with the symbols of the serpent, the double bent rod and the crescent. The ogham text reads IRATADDOARENS- but, as is usual with Pictish ogham inscriptions, it has not been interpreted.

An example of an inscription on a non-stone artifact is the eighth-century St Ninian's Isle chape, probably from a sword scabbard (Fig. 2.5). It is inscribed on both sides with texts that have been variously interpreted. One possibility is that they are to be read together as IN NOMINE DEUS RESAD FIL[I] SPIRITUS SANCTI O. 'In the name of God, of the Son, of the Holy Spirit. Resad'. The final letter O is presumably an error and RESAD a personal name,

Fig. 2.5 Chape from St Ninian's Isle, now in the National Museum of Antiquities of Scotland (photograph National Museum of Antiquities of Scotland)

probably that of the owner of the scabbard.

The Picts then inscribed texts on a wider variety of objects than did the south-west Britons. Another point of comparison between the inscriptions of south-west Britain and those of Pictland lends further support to the view that the Picts had a firmer grasp of literacy than did the south-west Britons. In Pictland, the two scripts, ogham and roman, generally occur on separate monuments and are used for different languages. Texts in Latin were inscribed in roman script, whether capital or insular, while texts in Pictish were inscribed in ogham. There are no certain exceptions to this rather rigid rule. It is true that the early Irish words *cross* 'cross' and *magg-* 'son' occur in some ogham texts but they occur as single words in the middle of Pictish sentences, presumably because they had been borrowed into the Pictish language. If IRE on the St Vigeans stone is interpreted as Gaelic *i ré,* this may also indicate Old Gaelic/Irish borrowing into the language. In general, however, texts in Pictish occur in ogham script, those in Latin in roman script. The existence of this pattern and the strictness with which it seems to have been applied suggest a level of literate awareness which is not demonstrable in south-west Britain.

In the south-west there are no stones containing only ogham texts and no pattern emerges from the bi-literal texts. The Lewannick stone, for example, has a Latin text in roman script with only the Irish personal name repeated in ogham. The Fardel stone contains four different texts, two in each script, where two are single names and two may be either names or be in Irish. A correlation between language and script similar to that in Pictland is not found in the south-west.

A further point of comparison concerns the use of Latin. There is evidence of a greater use of Latin in south-west Britain than in Pictland, in that it is the usual language of the inscribed texts whereas in Pictland the usual language is Pictish. This may be associated with Bede's well-known account of King Nechtan's reply to Ceolfrith of Jarrow that he and his people would follow Roman custom in so far as their remoteness from the Roman language and nation would allow it (*Historia Ecclesiastica* V. 21). As noted above, the Latin used in the south-west is an irregular, if not a sub-standard, variety of the language. The same seems to apply to the Latin used in the Pictish inscriptions. There are spellings like [E]TT for *et* and FIL[I] for *filii* and some of the confusion of the St Ninian's Isle text may well be due to linguistic errors in the Latin.

Although the two areas can be seen to be in some ways comparable in their production of inscriptions, it can be argued that literacy among the Picts was of a higher standard and more widespread than literacy among the south-west Britons. A question that we should ask of both communities concerns the audience that was anticipated for their inscriptions. From our literate twentieth-century perspective it would seem a waste of time, money and effort to produce an inscription that no-one could read. Yet it is straining credulity to imagine that most people in, say, the ninth or tenth century could walk up to a carved cross or cross-slab like Sancreed in Cornwall or Brechin in Pictland, read the text and understand it. Still less is this likely to be true of ogham inscriptions. Who then formed the intended audience for these inscriptions?

There would probably have been the occasional literate person, no doubt a priest or monk, who would perhaps have read aloud an inscribed text to other people. Some of the memorial stones, both those in ogham and those in roman script, could have been intended for that sort of audience in both areas. It may also have been that the inscribed texts were intended both for a human and for a divine audience. In view of the association between literacy and the church at this period, it would have been perfectly reasonable to assume that God and the saints were literate. If the saints in heaven knew someone's name then they could intercede for their soul. Of course it cannot be proved that the Picts or the south-west Britons argued in this way but we can speculate that they might have done so.

A further possibility is that inscriptions served a symbolic function. There might well have been people who, although illiterate, were able to recognise letters as writing. Literacy was associated with the church and, we presume, with others of high status in the community. Perhaps it was considered that an inscription raised a monument in status. The Brechin cross-slab discussed above is inscribed with a text labelling the carved figure of the Blessed Virgin. It is unlikely, with such a well-known figure, that the carving was labelled to aid its identification. Perhaps in this case the text was inscribed as a symbol to indicate the importance of the cross-slab, or of the subject matter, or of the commissioner of the monument, or of more than one of these.

We can conclude that in south-west Britain in the early Christian period there was a fairly tenuous hold on literacy. No manuscript records survive and were it not for the inscribed stones we would have concluded that Dumnonia was an illiterate society. These stones are relatively few in number considering that they were produced over some five or six centuries. Moreover, there is no surviving range of inscribed monuments, only stones, and most of them are rather crude pillar-stones. By contrast, literacy seems to have played a more important role in Pictish than in south-western society, even though there are no surviving manuscripts from Pictland either. A relatively larger number of inscribed monuments, considered per century, has survived, and these represent a wider range of artifacts. The inscriptions also exhibit a greater control of literate procedures with ogham script used for Pictish texts, roman script (both capital and cursive) for Latin texts.

We are not really accustomed to extolling the Picts for their high level of literacy, but perhaps we should be doing just this. Some ten years ago I suggested that the use of both capital and insular script amongst the non-ogham Pictish inscriptions might point to a relatively sophisticated and widespread writing tradition, and that this was likely to have been a manuscript tradition even though such manuscripts have by and large not survived (Okasha 1985, 48). If we consider, as some scholars do, that the Pictish symbols are a form of writing (in the broadest sense of the term), then these too may be taken as evidence of Pictish literacy. We cannot understand the Pictish ogham texts because we cannot understand the language and/or the spelling conventions; nor are we certain of the meanings of the symbols on the symbol stones. However it is surely unjustifiably arrogant of us to argue that because we are incompetent, the Picts were illiterate. We should perhaps give greater consideration to the idea of the Picts as a nation where literacy played a significant role in society.

Dept. of English
University College, Cork

References

Allen, J.R. and Anderson, J. 1903, *The Early Christian Monuments of Scotland.* Edinburgh.

Clancy, T.O. 1993, 'The Drosten Stone: a new reading', *PSAS* 123 (1993), 345-53.

Dark, K. 1992, 'Epigraphic, art-historical, and historical approaches to the chronology of Class I inscribed stones', in Edwards, N. and Lane, A. eds., *The Early Church in Wales and the West,* Oxford, 51-61.

Nash-Williams, V.E. 1950, *The Early Christian Monuments of Wales*. Cardiff.

Okasha, E. 1985, 'The Non-Ogam Inscriptions of Pictland', *Cambridge Medieval Celtic Studies,* 9 (1985) 43-69.

Okasha, E. 1993, *Corpus of Early Christian Inscribed Stones of South-west Britain.* Leicester.

Thomas, A.C. 1994, *And Shall These Mute Stones Speak? Post-Roman Inscriptions in Western Britain.* Cardiff.

Appendix

The texts of the inscriptions are given below, in the order in which they are discussed. The texts are transliterated with word-division spaces added, abbreviations expanded and incidental marks omitted. The following system of transliteration is used:

A indicates a legible letter A; [A] indicates a damaged letter, probably A; [.] indicates one lost letter, the number varying according to the number of dots; - indicates complete loss of text. A possible translation of each text is given inside inverted commas with damaged letters in square brackets and words added in round brackets.

Lanherne, text 1: RUNHOL 'Runhol'
text 2: BREID [ET] [I]MAH 'Breid [and] [I]mah'

Camborne: LEUIUT IUSIT HEC ALTARE PRO ANIMA SUA 'Leuiut ordered this altar for his own soul'

Welltown: [VA]ILAT[H]I [F]ILI VROCH[ANI] '(the stone) of [Va]ilat[h]us, son of Vroch[anus]'

Southill: CVMREGNI FILI MAVCI '(the stone) of Cumregnus, son of Maucus'

St Just: SELVS IC IACIT 'Selus lies here'

Lewannick: [HIC] IACIT VLC[A]GNI, '[here] lies (the body) of Ulc[a]gnus'

Nanscow: VLCAGNI FI[LI] SEVERI, '(the stone) of Ulcagnus, son of Severus'

Fardel, text 1: FANONI MAQVIRINI '(the stone) of Fanonus, (son) of Maqvirinus'
text 2: MAQIQICI '(the stone) of Maqiqicus'
text 3: SAFFAQQUCI '(the stone) of Saffaqqucus'
text 4: G[A]G[R]A[NV]I '(the stone) of G[a]g[r]a[nv]us'

Lanteglos: AELSEL[Đ] 7 GENE[REĐ] [W]O[H]TE ÞYS[N]E [S]YB[STEL] FOR AELWYNEYS S[O]UL 7 [F]OR HEY[SEL] 'Aelsel[đ] and Gene[ređ] made this ?family place (*or* place of peace) for Aelwyn's soul and for ?themselves (*or* Hey[sel])'

St Vigeans: DROSTEN IRE UORET [E]TT FORCUS 'Drosten in the reign of Uoret and Forcus'

Brechin: SANCTA MARIA MATER CHRISTI ‘St Mary, mother of Christ’

Brandsbutt: IRATADDOARENS- (uninterpreted)

St Ninian’s Isle: IN NOMINE DEUS RESAD FIL[I] SPIRITUS SANCTI ‘In the name of God, of the Son, of the Holy Spirit. Resad ‘

From Birsay to Tintagel : A Personal View

Christopher D Morris

Introduction

As an archaeologist concerned with the archaeology of the First Millenium AD, it has always irritated me that the term 'Dark Age' has survived. It is itself a relic of a text-dominated approach to the latter part of this period, which has in the past emphasised either the absence of written sources or the confused nature of them, such that one might have described the period as much in terms 'text-confused' as 'text-aided'! However, much light has now been shed not only by re-examination of the texts and other text-related disciplines (such as place-names), but most particularly by the disciplines concerned with material culture (archaeology and art-history). The period concerned has been illumined for some decades now by high quality scholarship on all fronts and deserves a more appropriate description. Terms such as 'Early Christian' and 'Early Historic' have been proposed in the past by notable scholars such as Charles Thomas and Leslie Alcock and certainly their currency in Ireland and Scotland respectively has been fairly widespread. However, neither term is entirely satisfactory as they have some 'value-laden' element embedded in them which tends to 'skew' the perception of the period, be it the dominance of the Church or the primacy of historical texts. It would seem far preferable to revert to a term which is simply period-descriptive and of widespread currency: Early Medieval.

Two of the places most frequently referred to in relation to the archaeology of the Early Medieval period in northern and western Britain are Birsay in Orkney and Tintagel in Cornwall (Fig. 1). It has been my privilege to undertake archaeological work in both areas in the past two decades. I have *indeed* gone from Birsay to Tintagel and the work that I shall describe here looks at both my older work at Birsay, now proceeding towards publication, and the more recent surveys and excavations at Tintagel, which are only at an interim stage. This is very much a "personal view" on aspects of two excavation campaigns over a number of years in two widely separated parts of Britain, although broadly contemporary. It will be concerned with three aspects:
1) the evidence, as we now understand it, for Birsay in the pre-Viking period, when I think we can reasonably claim it to be a power-centre of some importance;

2) a re-consideration of the previous proposition that it should be seen in the context of a 'Celtic monastery' model;
and 3) a brief review of the evidence from Tintagel, which has also been seen in such a context, and suggestions as to how we might now interpret it.

Birsay Bay

The Bay of Birsay is a marked indentation on the N W coast of Mainland Orkney (Fig. 3.1). It is, in fact, two bays, divided by a small promontory of land called the Point of Snusan or Snushan. The northernmost is the larger, bounded on the N by the Point of Buckquoy, which was originally attached to the Brough of Birsay, now separated by the 238m wide Brough Sound. This tidal island, projecting out into the Atlantic, is connected at low tide by a modern concrete track across the natural causeway of exposed rocks.

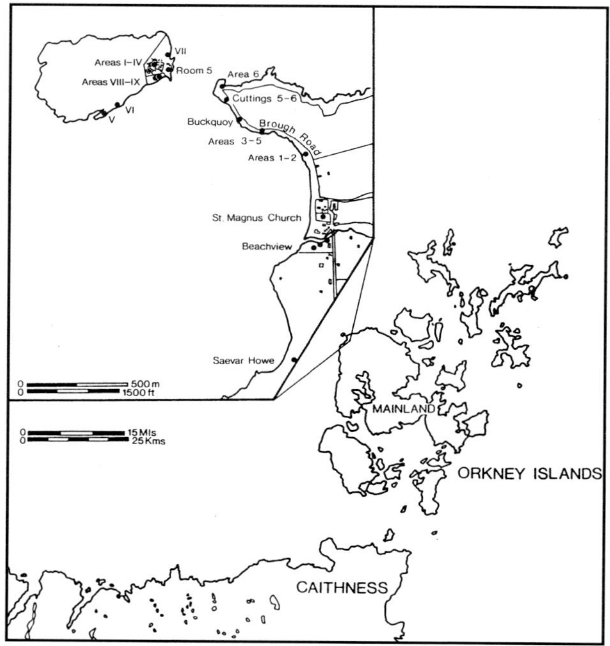

Fig. 3.1. Location of Birsay and sites around Birsay Bay (L McEwan after N Emery)

It is clear, as several writers have emphasised (Marwick 1952, 130-1; Crawford, B 1983, 116-7), that the name 'Birsay' is a contraction of the form *Byrgisherađ*, as found in *Orkneyinga Saga* (although the form *Byrgisey* is also found). The second element, *herađ* refers to the administrative district, later parish, of Harray, while the first is derived from *byrgi*, the i-umlaut form of ON *borg*, a fortress or stronghold. The term in the Faroe Islands "...is almost always used of narrow necks or steep cliffs or of enclosed places for sheep" (MacGregor, in Morris 1989 Chap 1.4), and this would be an entirely appropriate description for the first element of *Byrgisherađ*. Such a narrow neck of land might well have originally existed - rather as had clearly existed at the Brough of Deerness (Morris with Emery 1986, 309-10) - and perhaps represented on the 17th and 18th Century drawings of the Earl's Palace and Birsay (RCAHMS 1940, II, Figs 68 & 69, Pls 5 & 6 after 12).

Historical evidence indicates that in the past Birsay was a centre of both political and ecclesiastical power in Orkney second only to Kirkwall in the later Norse, Mediaeval and early Modern periods, but forerunner to that place in the Viking period. However, it is only with the accounts in the *Orkneyinga Saga* (*OS*), written *c.* 1192-1206, of the exploits of the later Viking Earls of Orkney that Birsay itself enters the historical record. Two entries concerning Earl Thorfinn in *c.* 1048 and *c.* 1065 (Taylor 1938 (ed), 188-189, 368, n 3) establish quite clearly that both the Earl's seat and the first Cathedral were in Birsay (*OS* chaps 31 and 32: Pálsson and Edwards 1978, 71). There has been much discussion as to the significance of the *Saga* entries for location and identification of these structures, and this has been well-rehearsed elsewhere (e.g. RCAHMS 1946, II, nos 1 & 6: 1-5 & 7; Radford 1959; 1962a & b; 1983; Cruden 1958; 1965; Lamb 1974; 1983; Cant 1983, 8-9). Birsay became the political and ecclesiastical power-centre of an Earldom, which extended N to Shetland, and S at the very least to Caithness, and at times probably far wider. Later, Birsay became an area particularly associated with Orkney's own martyr-saint, Magnus. The sequence of events concerned with his death, burial in the minster at Birsay and the subsequent miracles reported at his grave are re-told in some detail by the *Saga* writer, culminating in the translation of his relics to Kirkwall (*OS* chaps 52, 56 and 57: Pálsson and Edwards 1968, 88-9 and 94-9). Norse Christianity clearly focussed upon Birsay, but once Magnus's bones were transferred to Kirkwall, and the Cathedral was built there, naturally the focus of secular and ecclesiastical power was shifted away from Birsay.

Orkney in the Pre-Norse period: historical considerations

When we turn to the pre-Norse period, then from a strictly historical point-of-view, the picture in Birsay is *pre*-historic, for there are *no* documentary references whatsoever. However, at a more general level, it would be more accurate to decribe this period as *proto*-historic, for we have a certain amount of historical or quasi-historical evidence which can be cited in relation to the native people in "the Northern Isles" in the period up to the advent of the Norse. A late Scandinavian source, the *Historia Norvegiae*, described the islands as having been inhabited by "Picts and Papae" (Anderson (trans) 1922, I, 330-1; Crawford 1987, 3 & 56; Wainwright 1962, 99), the latter of whom appear to have left permanent reminders of their presence in place-names such as Papa Stour and Papil in Shetland and Papa Westray and Papdale in Orkney (MacDonald 1977; Crawford 1987, 165-7; Thomson 1987, 40).

To Nennius, writing *c.* 800AD, there was no doubt that Picts "occupied the islands which we call Orkney" (Morris J (ed & trans) 1980, 20), and a less reliable source, Claudian (chap 32: quoted in Wainwright 1962, 93), may be referring to Picts in Shetland. Recently, the re-discovery of the *Bern Chronicle* has confirmed that another eighth-century writer also believed that the Orkneys were the "islands of the Picts" (Dumville 1976), and, by implication, this may also have been the view of Gildas in the sixth century (Winterbottom (ed & trans) 1978, chaps 14 and 19).

Recent work on the Picts from an historical viewpoint would emphasise their heterogeneity at the time when they reach recorded history (i.e. 297 AD onwards), and it would now seem clear that they should be seen as a political (rather than ethnic) grouping opposed to Rome. My former colleague, Professor John Mann, has compared their existence and coming together, to that of "the fusion of people on the Continent, in the face of Roman power, into...great confederations..." (Mann 1974, 41; also see Breeze 1994). Bede's statement that

> "...all the peoples and kingdoms of Britain [were] divided among the speakers of four different languages, British, Pictish, Irish and English..." *(Historia Ecclesiastica (HE)* iii, 6: Colgrave and Mynors (ed & trans) 1969, 230-1)

indicates that by the seventh century the Picts were recognised to be one of the four great peoples of North Britain.

Even so, indications that the Orkney Picts may have acted as an independent unit (or as part of a "northern Pictish" grouping) seems clear from accounts of the putting down of a rebellion there in 682 AD by Bridei mac Bili (*Tigernach Annals* & *Annals of Ulster*: Anderson (trans) 1922, I, 191), and of the reference to an Orcadian *regulus* in *c.* 565 AD (Adamnan, II, 42: Anderson and Anderson (ed & trans) 1961, 440-3) in relation to a visit by St Columba of Iona to the court of Bridei mac Maelchon near Inverness and in the context of the voyage of Cormac, a follower, who

> "...attempted for the second time to seek a desert place in the ocean...[and] The saint ...foreknew in the spirit that after some months this Cormac would come to the Orcades. And it did afterwards so happen" (Anderson and Anderson (ed & trans) 1961, chap II, 42, 440-3).

In addition to the "mission" of Cormac, about twenty years later, the *Annals of Ulster* record one or two expeditions (there may be a scribal repetition) of King Aedan mac Gabrain to Orkney from Dalriada (*c.* 580 AD: Anderson (trans) 1922, i, 86). Certainly, with this background, there seems no reason to doubt the likely influence from the Columban church in the area of Northern Pictland.

However, there were other influences, the most obvious being that from Northumbria. After the Battle of Nechtanesmere on 20th May 685, the Northumbrians accepted a border - metaphorically at least - at the Firth of Forth and

> "The Picts now have a treaty of peace with the English and rejoice to share in the catholic peace and truth of the church universal..." (*HE* v, 23: Colgrave and Mynors (ed & trans) 1969, 560-1)

The apparent wish to "share in the catholic peace and truth" indicates a shift in ecclesiastical alignment on the part of the Picts towards the practice and outlook of the Northumbrian Church in the post-Synod of Whitby era. It is, therefore, unsurprising that in 710 AD Nechtan, King of the Picts, should have appealed to Ceolfrid, Abbot of Wearmouth-Jarrow, for guidance on the thorny subjects of the date of Easter and the form of tonsure. But, in addition:

> "He...asked for builders to be sent to build a church of stone in their country after the Roman fashion" (*HE* v, 21: Colgrave and Mynors (ed & trans) 1969, 532-5)

This Northumbrian influence can only have intensified in the period after 716 AD when the expulsion of the *familia* of Iona from Pictish territory took place.

Although there is no necessary connection with Orkney in the legend of a mission to Pictland by St Boniface, in the course of which 150 churches were built (Legend of St Boniface in Skene 1867; Skene 1876, i, 277; ii, 229), *a priori* it must be regarded as a distinct possibility that, if there is any historical basis for the legend, the mission would have included Orkney. It is difficult to assess the reliability and significance of both church dedications and particularly distinctive place-names, but it is sometimes assumed that the St Peter dedications of churches relate in part to this phase of activity. The single Boniface dedication (on Papa Westray), and the group of *Peterkirk* dedications have been taken to be of this period in Orkney, and may also link up with the St Tredwell (Triduana) dedication, also on Papa Westray (Thomson 1987, 9-10; Lamb 1995). William Thomson has suggested that:

> "At the very least, it demonstrated the presence of a cult which had its base in Northumbrian territory, and suggests links between the Orkney Papae and a Northumbrian mission to Pictland" (Thomson 1987, 10)

Going further, Dr Raymond Lamb has suggested that all this argues for, and is paralleled by, a Carolingian form of ecclesiastical organisation (Lamb 1993). It also gives a more credible context for the occurrence of the *Papa* type place-names than the suggestion of an eremitical movement to remote situations - which manifestly in several cases they were not (MacDonald 1977; Lowe 1988, Appendix 3; Thomson 1987, 40; Lamb 1993).

Thus, although there are no documentary references to Birsay as such during this period, we may be sure that pre-Norse archaeological material found

during the course of archaeological investigation is most likely to relate to a context of the historical Picts, and in particular to an Orcadian sub-group of the Picts. This Pictish sub-group, however, is also likely to have had connections with both the Dalriadic and Northumbrian political and, more particularly, ecclesiastical and cultural spheres of influence.

Birsay in the Pictish period: the archaeological evidence

In the absence of specific documentary evidence for the status of Birsay in the pre-Norse period, we may now gather together the results from the various more recent archaeological investigations for an up-to-date characterisation of the material evidence for the Pictish period in Birsay Bay.

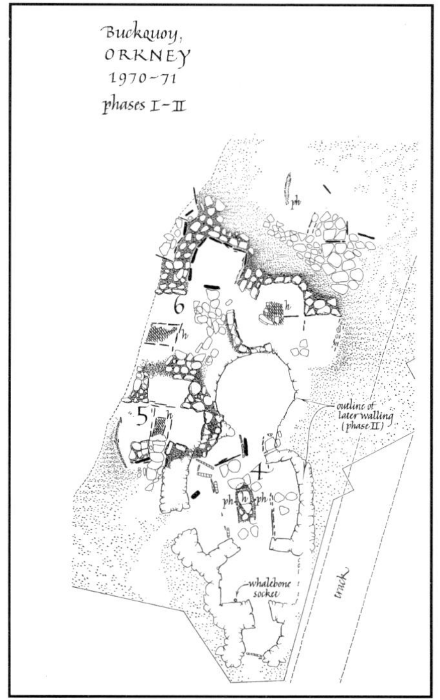

Fig. 3.2a. Buckquoy: plan of Phases I-II (I G Scott, Crown copyright)

Settlements and Houses

Naturally, pride of place must go to the breakthrough in understanding of Pictish settlement types. Although her interpretation of later sequences has been somewhat controversial, the Pictish phases at the site called "Buckquoy" excavated by Dr Anna Ritchie have provided clear examples of distinctive buildings in each phase of activity. The early Pictish houses at Buckquoy were both of a cellular form, one being trefoil and the other with five cells (Ritchie 1977, 176, fig 2), (Fig. 3.2a) although the exterior forms were quite likely to be oval (Ritchie 1989, 47). The later Pictish farmstead on the Buckquoy site was far more elaborate, even prompting the description "almost anthropomorphic" (Ritchie 1974, 27;

Ritchie 1977, 183; Ritchie 1983, 56). (Fig. 3.2b). This form is certainly a sophisticated one, in contrast to the "cellular" forms, and was immediately related to similar buildings found by Dr Iain Crawford at the Udal, North Uist, as well as other, less well-recorded or understood sites in the north (Ritchie 1974, 26-9; see Crawford, I A, 1974).

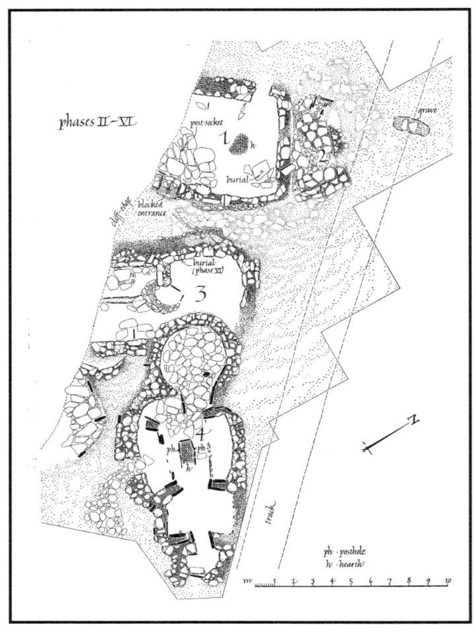

Fig. 3.2b. Buckquoy: plan of Phases II-VI (I G Scott, Crown copyright)

When the site of Buckquoy was seen as an isolated domestic site in the area of Birsay, questions obviously arose as to its status in relation to the Brough of Birsay (Ritchie 1983, 54) and the excavator postulated that "it is possible that Buckquoy functioned as the home farm for the community living on the Brough" (Ritchie 1985, 198). Even so, this excavated site was largely seen as an isolated site between the two well-known *foci* on the Brough and in the village area of Birsay. Since that time, from Birsay Bay, two clear examples of buildings in this tradition have been excavated, with possibly several others which survived only in fragmentary form.

A figure-of-eight-shaped building has been discovered at Red Craig (see Morris 1989, Chaps 6 & 7.3 - 7.6), a mere 90-100m away from Buckquoy. This building remained substantially intact, being eliptical in shape, with an internal figure-of-eight shape (Fig. 3.3). Two rooms were thus created, and the entrance was in the S wall of the W room, stepping down from a flagged threshold to some internal flagging. There may have been a possible hearth at the E end of Room A, but there were clearly two fire-pits in Room B and a stone - lined gulley. Against the E wall of Room B was added what is interpreted as an oven. From the later phases of collapse, and the absence of internal roof - supports, it is deduced that the building was constructed in corbel - fashion, and in one

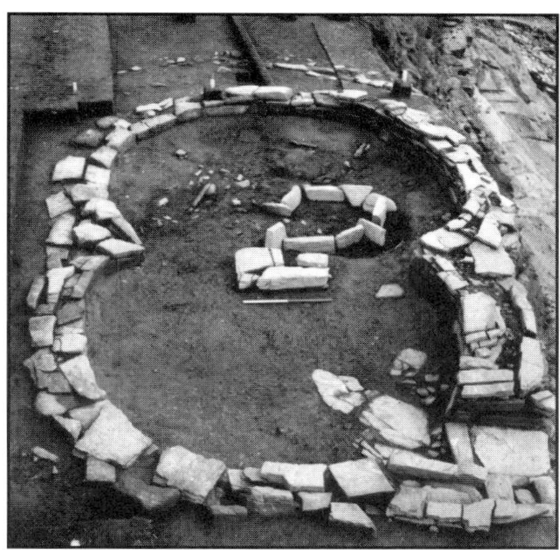

Fig. 3.3. Red Craig (Area 3): photograph of main structure from W (C D Morris, Crown Copyright)

area of the site - to the E - there was some evidence for the presence of a surrounding *annulus* (Area 4, Phase A). It would thus seem that a hollow had been deliberately created in the natural subsoil, which was lined with stones. In this case, a substantial horizontally-coursed wall was created on the inside, and, despite later destruction, it would seem that there was then an encircling bank of clay with further walling forming a rim or edge to this. Final publication has stressed that, while its internal form is distinctive (its nearest parallel in shape, and possibly construction, being the double *clochan* at Reask in Co Kerry), this is likely to be a variation upon a common theme, with a less distinguished exterior appearance as at Buckquoy (Morris 1989, chap 6 esp 171-2 & chap 10, 287).

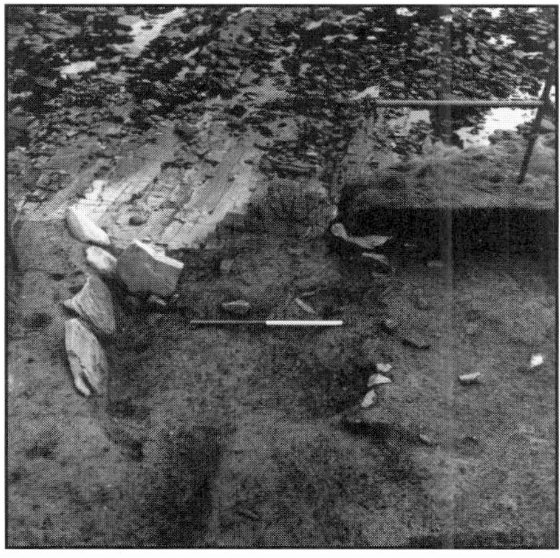

Fig. 3.4a. Red Craig (Area 5): photograph of remains of second structure from N (C D Morris, Crown copyright)

The remnants of what is assumed to be a second building of a form perhaps similar to the circular cell at the "head" end of the late Pictish building at Buckquoy was also uncovered on this site (see Morris 1989, chap 6, esp 189 & chap 10, 283-5) (Fig. 3.4). It consisted of a "scoop" into the natural subsoil which had been lined with stones

Fig. 3.4b. Red Craig (Area 5): photograph of partition within second structure from W (C D Morris, Crown copyright)

to create a circular room; this was divided off from what presumably was the main room by a partition represented by three "socket" holes originally filled with vertical slabs. The constructional method for the circular room, with vertical slabs, is reminiscent of the Late Pictish building at Buckquoy (Ritchie 1977).

It does not seem unreasonable to interpret the two buildings together as a small farming-unit, with perhaps a yard to be implied to the S of the figure-of-eight shaped building, but now destroyed by erosion. Dating cannot be provided by the artefactual material, but fortunately carbonised seed from one of the fire-pits (Phase A) produced a radiocarbon date range of AD 600-915. Usage of, and modification to, the figure-of-eight shaped building was noted: the fire-pits in Room A were replaced by a hearth constructed of upright flagstones. Perhaps more significant in structural terms was the construction of what appears to have been a solid stone partition wall between Rooms A and B, with a passage to both N and S. It may well have also had a structural function, as roof - support, but there was insufficient stratigraphical evidence to support the idea that it may have been a fire - or hearth - back at this period.

It is to be noted that there are few characteristically "Pictish" artefacts; indeed the only artefact from Red Craig that parallels the Buckquoy collection is a stone gaming-board from Phase C. Also, one might be able to argue from the *absence* of clearly identifiable Norse cultural attributes in the artefact assemblage from the early phases - no steatite, antler combs or bone pins. Negative evidence is always difficult to sustain in argument, however, at least it may be a pointer, for on sites a short distance to the S, more characteristically Viking-age artefacts *were* present above the earlier phases. Radiocarbon dates for the later phases are AD 600-910 (Phase C: occupation) and AD 875-1055 (Phase E: disuse). This would then imply that the construction and occupation of the structure should be dated to the Late Pictish and Early Viking periods, and its disuse clearly to the Viking period proper.

The nature and parallels of the structural forms are crucial to identification of cultural context. It is now a commonplace that Pictish-period house forms are cellular in form, be they "radial" or "axial" (Hunter 1986, 26) and that they contrast markedly with the buildings of the Scandinavian incomers (Crawford 1987, 140-6, esp Fig 46). Despite the likely exterior form as an oval, it is quite evidently the case that the Red Craig building is related to this native "cellular" tradition, a tradition that can also be seen in a group of such buildings at the Point of Buckquoy, originally examined by F T Wainwright (see Morris 1989, Chap 4).

Recent work by Dr John Hunter on the Brough of Birsay produced a series of primary features interpreted as structural remnants from his "Phase 1". Although all these features on Sites VII, VIII and IX imply "cellular" structures, only sufficient remained on Site VII with structures 19 & 20 for convincing reconstruction (Hunter 1986, Chap 2, esp 39-45 & 61-4) (Figs. 3.5 and 3.6). Further structural remains excavated by Morris on the Brough of Birsay, identified by the presence of primary features, such as post-holes below Norse buildings on Site IV South, or gulleys around buildings whose walls had been removed on Area I, appear to date from the pre-Viking period, from the presence of an ogam stone (see below) and insular metalwork (Morris 1981 & 1982; Hunter 1983, 155-6; Morris forthcoming a). Radiocarbon dates are consistent with this, giving a range at 2-sigma level from early seventh to late eighth century.

It is notable that the two date ranges accepted above for Phases A and C at Red Craig are consistent with the overall range obtained from Sites VII and IX on the Brough of Birsay (from AD 640 +/- 60 to AD 828 +/- 70). No radiocarbon dates were utilised at Buckquoy; but the Late Pictish period dating derived from artefacts and retrospective chronology relative to the Norse phases (Ritchie 1977, 192) is internally consistent and does not conflict with other historical or cultural considerations. Overall, the overwhelming probability is that all three sites are contemporary and reflect the same Late Pictish period cultural milieu.

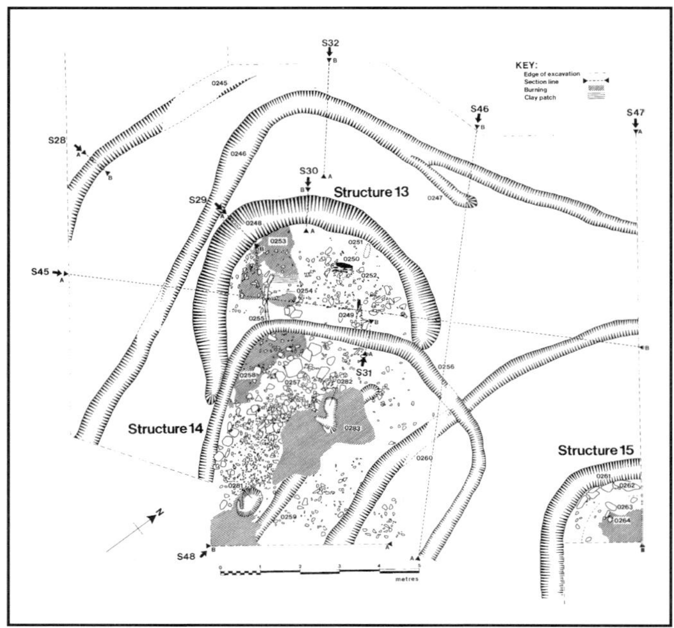

Fig. 3.5. Brough of Birsay (Site IX): plan of Phase 1 structures 13, 14 & 15 (J R Hunter, Crown copyright)

It thus seems clear that what seemed rather extraordinary in Birsay in 1971-2 (see Ritchie 1983, 63) has now been shown to be a norm, as cellular buildings have continued to be excavated both from this area and further afield: the Howe, near Stromness (Hedges and Bell 1980; Carter *et al* 1984; Neil 1985; Ritchie 1985, 201-2; Smith 1990, esp Illus 4.2b & f, 35 & 36-9); the Broch of Gurness (RCAHMS 1946, II, no 263, 75-9, esp figs 129 and 132; Ritchie 1974, 26, fig 1; Hedges 1987, II, 65-71, 83-6 184; Ritchie 1989, 46-8); the Calf of Eday (Hunter 1986, 43-5; also see Ritchie 1985, 196 & 201); Yarrows and the Wag of Forse, in Caithness (Ritchie 1974, 26-7 & 32); Carlungie, Angus (Alcock 1984, 12-14 & 18); and the Western Isles (Armit 1990, 64-8; Harding and Armit 1990, 91-2 & 98-106).

At the other end of the spectrum are rectangular or subrectangular buildings of this period: the late Peter Gelling drew attention to rectangular buildings and paving excavated under his direction at Skaill, Deerness (Gelling

1984, 12-15 & 36; Gelling 1985), and examples at the Wag of Forse and Nybster in Caithness and Gurness in Orkney are among comparative structures brought forward by Ritchie (1974, 26-7 & 32) and Alcock (1984, 12 & 18-19). More recently, Beverley Smith has drawn attention, among the variety of forms at the Howe, to a small rectangular building (Smith 1990, Illus 4.2e & 37).

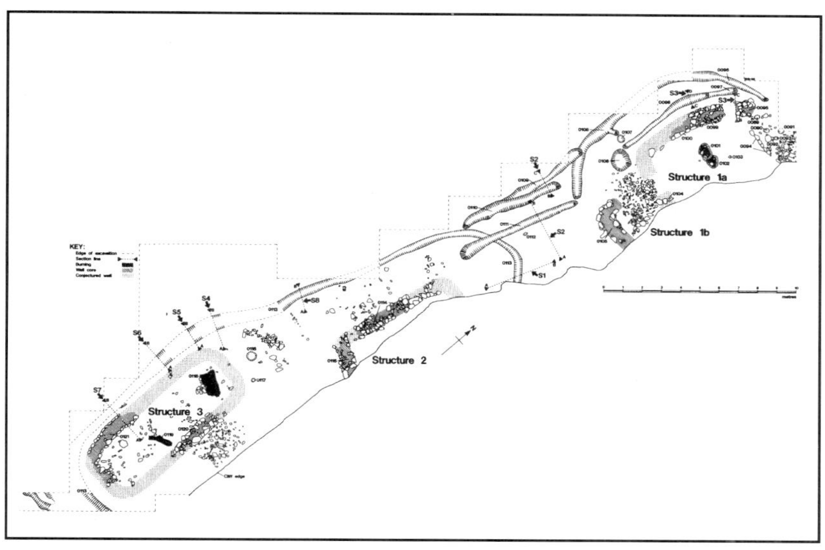

Fig. 3.6. Brough of Birsay (Site VII): plan of Phase 1 structures 19 & 20 (J R Hunter, Crown copyright)

When Alcock reviewed the traditions of building of the period, he suggested that there were two traditions: "circular" and "axial" (Alcock 1984, 18). As Ritchie has implied, this is likely to be an over-simplified division:

> "It seems likely that these various house-types represent inter-related architectural development rather than separate traditions, and the impression given by the existing dating evidence is that the development is linear and sequential from wheelhouses onwards" (Ritchie 1985, 201)

Certainly, although the Buckquoy-related type of building can be more readily recognised, it is clear that there were also buildings akin to wheelhouse structures at sites from Shetland to the Western Isles which are relevant to at least a discussion of the "proto-Picts" (Alcock 1984, 14-19; Ritchie 1985, 201), as well as circular structures on erstwhile souterrain sites (Watkins 1980; Watkins 1984, Maxwell 1987). Recently, John Hunter has drawn attention to "...the nucleus of the later Iron Age settlement from the 5th Century AD...constructed...from an extant souterrain-type building..." at Pool, Sanday (Hunter 1990, 181). In between the two extremes lie the "irregular housing 'blocks', with oval and sub-rectangular rooms" from Howe and Pool, Sanday (Ritchie 1989, 48; Smith 1990, Illus 4.2d, e & f & 37-9; Hunter 1990, 183-5 & esp Illus 10.6). The structures identified by Hedges at Saevar Howe in Birsay Bay (Hedges 1983, 78-81), fit more easily into this tradition, and it must be remembered that some of the buildings, such as perhaps at Jarlshof in Shetland, may have been workshops and storehouses rather than dwellings (Ritchie 1989, 48-9). The complexity of the situation is best appreciated by reference to the recently-published report on the Orcadian multi-period site of Howe (Smith (ed) 1994, Chap 5). However, it is worth noting (as Hunter did), that at present, apart from Saevar Howe, the Birsay sites are 'detached', self-standing units, in contrast to the 'clustered' complexes at Pool (Hunter 1990, 179-91), Howe (Smith 1990; Smith (ed)1994) and, by implication, Cnip and Loch na Berie (Armit 1990; Harding and Armit 1990).

Symbol Stones and Graves

The symbol stone on the Brough of Birsay was originally thought to be associated with a triple-grave (Radford 1959, 17; Radford 1962b, 168; Cruden 1965, 25). Now, thanks to Mrs Curle's detective-work, this latter is clearly not the case (Curle 1982, 91-2; Ritchie, J N G and Fraser, I 1994, 19; Ritchie, A, 1986, 12). However, we may legitimately wonder whether, in fact, since it was found in pieces, but in association with a cemetery, it had originally been related to some other grave-monument(s)? In the light of more recent work, for instance at Dunrobin Castle, Sutherland (Close-Brooks 1980; Close-Brooks 1984), and Watenan, Caithness (Gourlay 1984), Close-Brooks has concluded that there is "...more and more circumstantial evidence that Pictish symbol stones were gravestones" (Close-Brooks 1984, 107; also see Ashmore 1980, 352).

It now seems clear that there was another Pictish stone also from Birsay: a decorated stone covered one of the short cists in the cemetery overlying the ruined broch mentioned above at Oxtro, with "the figure of an *eagle*...boldly cut" (Petrie 1873, 76-8). Although now lost, this seems best explained as a Pictish symbol-stone (Wainwright 1962, 93-4; Ritchie, J N G 1969; Ritchie, A 1985, 188 & 190-1; Morris 1989,24). Presumably it was re-used at Oxtro, but would have been a separate monument originally.

The symbol stone on the Brough of Birsay was associated with the lower stratum of burials in a cemetery seen by earlier excavators as pre-dating not merely the upper stratum of Norse Christian graves but the Viking period as a whole (Cruden 1958, 160; 1965, 23-5; Radford 1959, 17-18; 1962, 11; Curle 1982, 13). The graves took the form of long-cist burials with horizontal slabs and, in many cases, small head- or foot-stones. These graves were also seen as associated with structural remains below both the later chapel and the Norse churchyard enclosure, and the 'Celtic' nature of the remains appeared to be reinforced by the presence of what was taken to be a *leacht* (Cruden 1965, 24-5; Radford 1959, 17-18; 1962a, 11 & Plate II). Although a number of these assertions might now be questioned, there can be little doubt that there was a major cemetery of the Pictish period located on the Brough of Birsay.

The edge of part of a Late Iron Age and Pictish cemetery was excavated under rescue excavation conditions in Areas 1 and 2 on the Brough Road South of Red Craig (see Morris 1989, Chaps 5; 7.1-7.2; 7.6 & 9). On top of the naturally-deposited sand at the base of the excavations were set two stone cairns over human burials. Cairn 2, the more completely preserved example, demonstrated the construction method. A stone cist (in this case incomplete) had been set in the underlying sand, with an extended inhumation on a NNW-SSE orientation, placed on its side (Figs. 3.7a & 3.7b).Over this was heaped a layer of clean, barren sand, and then a mound of irregular stones and sand, which were faced with an outer kerbing of horizontally-coursed sandstone slabs, seven or eight courses high. No grave-goods were found in association with this burial, which was of a mature, possibly elderly, male. Cairn 1, much less well-preserved, but apparently of similar form, covered a cist (of much better construction than that under Cairn 2) in which two burials had been placed. The lower was probably an adult male, the upper an individual of about 18 years of age, whose sex is unclear. Only the lower halves of the bodies remained, due to erosion, but it was nevertheless likely that the lower torso had been covered with a shroud, weighted down with pebbles; and that the upper lay upon a slab over sand infill above the lower body. No grave-goods were found with either skeleton.

Fig. 3.7a. Brough Road South of Red Craig (Area 1): photograph of Cairn 2 (C D Morris, Crown copyright)

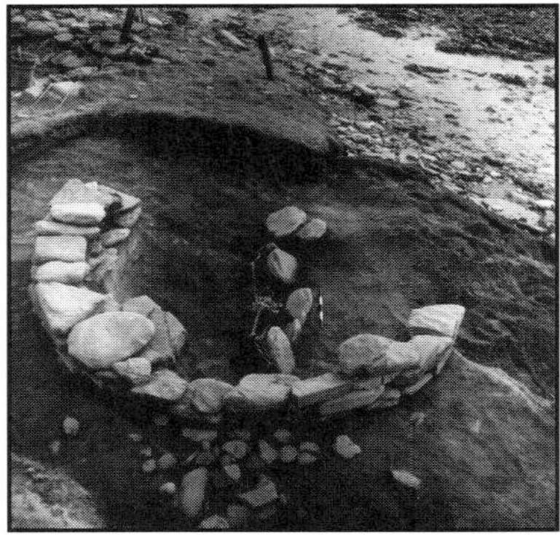

Fig. 3.7b. Brough Road South of Red Craig (Area 1): photograph of cist-grave exposed below Cairn 2 (C D Morris, Crown copyright)

In the absence of characteristic artefacts, dating is completely reliant upon the radiocarbon determinations. From these, the graves south of Red Craig were clearly to be associated with the earlier Pictish/Roman Iron Age. The dates of the three skeletons are quite conclusive: AD 55-570;AD 230-570; AD 245-585 (Morris 1989, 288 and 299), and are internally consistent so that the Roman Iron Age and earlier part of the Pictish period are involved here. It seems reasonable to accept the implication of the radiocarbon dates in cultural terms, and to describe these as "Pictish" burials. The recovery of isolated human bones, some of which at least are earlier than, or contemporary with, these cairns, justify the description of this overall as a Pictish cemetery. Phases B and C above the burials produced no diagnostic artefacts, but are given a *terminus ante quem* by the radiocarbon date-range of AD 620-890 for Phase D1 in this Area. There need, therefore, be no difficulty with locating them in the Pictish period. The dating of the burials south of Red Craig fits in with those obtained by radiocarbon for comparable sites (see Close-Brooks 1984, Appendix 1), most recently from Sandwick, Unst, Shetland (Bigelow 1984 and 1985).

The form of the graves was quite distinctive, and is now recognised as a distinctive form, particularly associated with the northern Pictish area

(Ritchie 1974, 31-2; Ashmore 1980; Close-Brooks 1984). Here the Pictish tradition appears to have been that of long-cist burial below mounds surmounted by well-constructed kerbed cairns, whether rectangular or circular. It has been suggested that the circular form (here and as already identified at Keiss, Ackergill and Watenan in Caithness, Garbeg and others) may be earlier than the rectangular (such as at Dunrobin and Sandwick) and that the latter may have been in usage amongst the Picts when they came into contact with the Norse - perhaps prompting "borrowing" of the form (Close-Brooks 1984). The long-cist form is ubiquitous in relation to these cairns, and the mound of sterile sand a common feature.

The long-cist form of burial is also a contemporary tradition that was followed in cemeteries where no cairns were constructed. In the light of the association of isolated long-cist burials with cairns at some of the sites now clearly identified as Pictish period cemeteries, it seems reasonable to interpret the feature from Cutting 3 on the Brough Road in similar terms, and to assume that the isolated human bones found through the early deposits of Area 1 may have come from similar burials. A similar isolated cist grave was excavated by Dr Ritchie at her Buckquoy site (Ritchie 1977, 183-4; 1983, 61-2), and it is notable that Pictish period slab-lined graves, dated by radiocarbon (although the details are not presently available), have recently been identified from Westness, Rousay (Kaland 1993, 312-4).

Ogam Inscriptions

So far, seven Orcadian Pictish period ogam inscriptions have been found, with four coming from the Birsay area (Ritchie 1983, 52-3; 1985, 191-2; Hunter 1990, 185-6). Two recorded from the Brough of Birsay in the past have uncertain original locations (Radford 1959, 5; Radford 1962b, 174; Cruden 1965, 25; Ritchie 1985, 192), but the location of another is certain, having been found during excavations directed by the writer on Area IV South (Morris 1981, 36; Morris 1982a, Plate 41) (Fig. 3.8). The fourth is on the, by now well-known, sandstone spindle whorl from Dr Ritchie's site at Buckquoy (Ritchie 1977, 181-2, 197, fig 8 no 84, 199, 221). It is interesting that this particular one was on a portable object, and Ritchie wonders if it is to be explained in terms of talismanic or magical connotations (Ritchie 1985, 192). But it is worth noting - as Oliver Padel has done (referred to in Ritchie 1985, 192) - that the object upon which this inscription had been placed was indeed one of everyday use, for which he coined the phrase "chattel inscription".

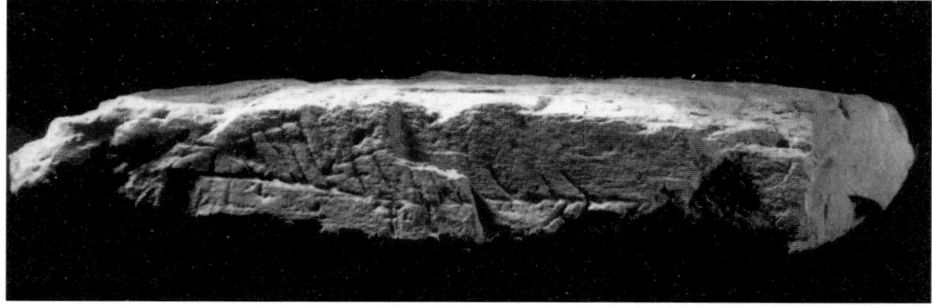

Fig. 3.8. Brough of Birsay (Site IV South): stone with ogam inscription (T Middlemass, Crown copyright)

It has been suggested in the past that all appear to be an unintelligible mixture of letters and therefore, as suggested by Jackson (1977; also in Hunter 1990, 186), they were conveying the older, non-Indo-European, form of the Pictish language. If we were to take up the implications of Padel's "chattel inscriptions", we might infer that there was a widespread knowledge of ogam at some period in the Pictish period (Padel *op cit*), and especially north of the Dornoch Firth (Wainwright 1962, 95-7). As for dating, that from Buckquoy has been placed in the early eighth century (Jackson 1977), in common with others from Orkney, although the earlier discoveries of inscriptions in Birsay might even come from a ninth-century Viking Age context (Ritchie 1985, 192). The recent find from Pool is dated to the sixth century (Hunter 1990, 185), and equally that from Birsay is from a clearly pre-Viking context, sealed by a rubble spread dated by radiocarbon to AD 560-769.

The Birsay ogams have recently been re-examined and re-interpreted by Dr Katherine Forsyth, and I gratefully acknowledge her comments, taken from ongoing work which should be consulted for full details, as follows:

1. The Buckquoy spindle whorl, with the inscription ENDDACTANIM-, is now interpreted by her as "a blessing on the soul of L", in the Old Irish language and manifestly Christian in sentiment. Both the Irish and Christian connotations have important implications which she has discussed in detail (Forsyth forthcoming a).
2. The group of three inscriptions on slabs from the Brough of Birsay appear to be carved on stones, perhaps from walls of structures on the site, although we do not have sufficient evidence to assert that they are contemporary, and

they are carved by different hands. They are described by Dr Forsyth as "informal graffiti", with perhaps fragments of personal names involved, of which Birsay 3 (from my own excavations) is the most intelligible, perhaps even referring to a name such as 'Mac-Onchon', as recorded in the Book of Leinster. Again, the indications are that the inscriptions are likely to be Irish in origin (Forsyth forthcoming b).
3. A small pebble may also have ogam characters (Curle 1982, 120), but this has yet to be verified by Dr Forsyth.

It is quite obvious that this re-evaluation is very important, implying as it does an Irish linguistic presence in the Birsay Bay area in the seventh and eighth centuries. It is also important in relation to the possible influence of the Columban church mentioned above, and the tradition of St Findan and Orkney (see Morris 1990, 7, with references).

Bells

Another, apparently distinctive artefact type recognised in Birsay, is the bronze-bound iron bell: two have been found. The hand-bell is normally associated with an ecclesiastical context and seen as a reflection of the activities of the church in the 'Celtic' areas of Britain and Ireland (Anderson 1881, 167-215). More recent work by Cormac Bourke on Irish, Welsh and Scottish examples suggests that, when found outside Ireland, they reflect the influence of the Irish church (Bourke 1980; 1983). The nineteen from Scotland (of which fourteen are iron) perhaps then reflect Irish missionary activity mediated through Iona (Bourke 1983, 466). The example from Saevar Howe is quite well-known, having been found in the nineteenth century (Farrer 1862; see Batey and Morris 1983, 85 and 97-8) (Fig. 3.9). Now, however, we know that the context for the bell is no longer so clear as the nineteenth-century account and interpretation would seem to indicate. This implies connection with an Early Christian burial-ground, and deposition with the advent of the Vikings to the area (Anderson 1881, 170-1; also see Cruden 1965, 25). Hedges's re-excavation demonstrates quite clearly that the cemetery post-dates the Viking and Pictish buildings on a settlement-mound site (Hedges 1983, *passim*), although the precise context of the bell as found in the nineteenth century within this is unclear. It may either be associated with the later cemetery (Morris 1983, 141) or be distinct from this cemetery and thus possibly be earlier (Hedges

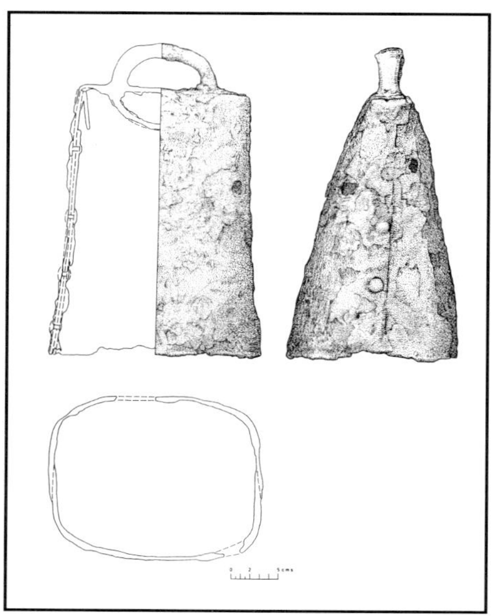

Fig. 3.9. Saevar Howe, Birsay: drawing of iron bell (H Jackson, Crown copyright)

1983, 120-1). Some support for the later dating possibility might be given by the evidence of the second example from the Brough of Birsay, apparently from a Lower Norse horizon (Curle 1982, 50-2; Curle 1983,77-8). However, it should be noted that the context for this is in a hearth of a building of some sophistication (Room VI), dated by Radford and Cruden to the eleventh century (Radford 1959, 19-20; Cruden 1958, 160-2; 1965, 29-31). Since the context must surely be secondary, as with Saevar Howe, the bell could still be early and from the Pictish period.

Other distinctive artefacts

Some time ago, Dr Anna Ritchie asserted that the painted pebble was not only associated with the Picts, but more particularly with those in Caithness, Orkney and Shetland (Ritchie 1972). Subsequently, two further finds have been made from the broch of Burrian on North Ronaldsay (MacGregor 1974, 100) and her own site in Birsay at Buckquoy (Ritchie 1977, 182, fig 8, no 87; Ritchie 1983, 58-9; Ritchie 1985, 200).

Another distinctive type of find recorded from Birsay was a group of stone gaming-boards: three from Buckquoy (Ritchie 1977, 187, figs 9 & 10), and one from the site of Red Craig mentioned above (Batey 1989, 220-1). The context from Red Craig is likely to be Late Pictish/ Early Viking (Morris 1989, 284 286), whereas that for the stratified example from Buckquoy is the midden associated with the early Norse farmstead (Ritchie 1977, 187). Another board of whalebone was found on the Brough of Birsay from the Middle Norse horizon (Curle 1982, 76, Ill 50 & 110). Of some interest here is Sterckx's conclusion that, whereas the game represented can be related to the Celtic game of *brandubh*, it is also essentially the same as Scandinavian *hnefatafl* (Sterckx 1970; 1973a; 1973b). Could it have been adopted by the incoming Scandinavians from the native Picts, and thereafter spread throughout the Viking world?

Evidence for fine metal-working and other crafts

On the Brough of Birsay, the excavations below Room 5 in the area to the east of the church have demonstrated that the lowest phase, stratigraphically, contained clear evidence for metalworking (Hunter and Morris 1982). This can, as shown in the report, be dated to the Pictish period, on grounds of both radiocarbon dates and other associated artefacts. This then has provided a context for Mrs Curle to analyse the material collected previously from the site, and her Phase plans for the area to the east of the chapel (Curle 1982, 15-17, Ill 5) demonstrates clear evidence for Pictish working "zones". Crucibles, slags and moulds from "Zone 5" were related to the evidence of moulds etc from previous excavations (Curle 1982, 26-44). One of the brooch-moulds from below Room 5 (no 300: Curle 1982, 26-7, Ill 13 & 14) can be related specifically to the metalwork from St Ninian's Isle - as can other moulds. Moulds for other copper-alloy objects, including multiple pin moulds (which match bone pins found below Room 5) and ornamental pins, have been found, with a significant concentration around a small well. The overall impression is that "Birsay must have been an important centre of bronze-casting before the arrival of the Norsemen..." (Curle 1982, 26-7). Similarly, a noteworthy lead disc, which might have been used for *cire perdue* casting (Curle 1974; Curle 1982, 48-9), crucibles and tuyeres reinforce this impression (also see Curle 1983, 71-7). From the recent excavations a fine gilded bronze mount, with clear parallels with Northumbrian material of the pre-Viking period, has been recovered (Morris 1982, Illus 42; Cronyn, Morris and Owen 1983).

Although there is no debris from glass-making activities, an amount of evidence is present which might suggest small-scale craft activity using glass, for instance in bead-making or inlay-work in metalwork (Hunter 1982, 46-7): glass mounts and a waster, vessel-glass (from both earlier and more recent excavations) and a *tessera* are noteworthy in this context.

Overall assessment

As is clear from this review, there is a considerable amount of archaeological evidence to demonstrate the importance of the Birsay area in the Pictish period.

Since there are no historical sources which refer to this, we can but infer that the range and quality of the material testifies to a focus of settlement and, conceivably, power - as it was later to become in the Viking and later Norse periods. In the Birsay Bay Project, the major contribution at one level has been to widen the archaeological context for other sites: to "create an archaeological perspective for the area" (Ritchie, 1983, 63). The buildings and internal occupation debris from Red Craig provide a contemporary parallel for the Late Pictish settlement at Buckquoy. They also emphasise, along with Hunter's recent work on the Brough of Birsay, the variety of the cellular structural forms of this period. In addition, they suggest a different picture of the distribution of farming settlements at this time, for the two sites are barely 100m apart, and that at the Point of Buckquoy, a further c. 100m away. Hitherto, the main evidence from the Bay for Pictish period burials has been the (essentially unpublished) late Christian cemetery on the Brough. The cairn-burials and long-cists from S of Red Craig appear to date from the early Pictish period, rather than the later, and are, therefore, an addition to the archaeological data-base, widening the chronological range.

The changed overall picture of Pictish and Viking settlement in the Bay that necessarily derives from the work of the Project as a whole is of major importance to the question of the inter-relationship of the native Picts to the incoming Norse in Scotland, as Birsay is so often seen as a key area (see Ritchie 1983; 1985, 191-198; Morris 1985, 216-221; Crawford B E, 1987, 155-88). This is not the place in which to explore this theme, but we may note that, on the general level, Thomson has speculated that the Scandinavian Earldom of Orkney may represent the takeover of a pre-existing entity, represented archaeologically by the presence north of the Dornoch Firth of the distinctive ogam stones and distinctive Pictish symbols (and burial forms?), and linguistically by the absence of *pit* place-names (Thomson 1987, 5-6). On the specific level of Birsay, it may be possible to speculate further that the Pictish focus here may have provided the basis for the later Norse Earls' establishment.

Although for much of their *recorded* history, the Picts were concerned with events to the south or west (i.e. as they impinged upon the Anglo-Saxon Northumbrians or Dalriadic Scots), and much of the monumental and archaeological evidence is concerned with areas such as Fife and Angus, as is now patently clear, they also had a northern focus. Professor Leslie Alcock (1984, 9-10), perhaps over-influenced by Professor Kenneth Jackson (1955), has contrasted the so-called "peripheral" Picts of Northern Scotland and the Northern Isles, with the so-called "heartland" Picts, so that the former supposedly had "a diluted Pictish or Proto-Pictish culture". However, as Dr Anna Ritchie has observed, Orkney was no more peripheral than Angus at times in the sixth or seventh centuries (1983; 1985), when the Moray Firth (i.e. the Inverness area) appears to have been the centre of the Pictish realm (Henderson 1971; 1975). Indeed, some of the finest examples of the Pictish sculptured stone series are to be found in this area (Curle 1940; Henderson 1958; Close-Brooks 1989; Henderson 1990). The work of the last two decades in Orkney - and particularly Birsay - have now amply demonstrated that conventional views of "centre" and "periphery" must now be re-assessed for the Pictish period in northern Britain. The "Northern Isles" of Shetland and Orkney were integral to the Pictish cultural, and presumably political, orbit and Birsay would appear to be a major power-centre within this.

The Church and 'The Celtic Monastery'

Some time ago, Dr Ralegh Radford emphasised the place of Orkney in the overall story of "The Celtic Monastery in Britain" (Radford 1962a). His wide-ranging discussion took in Ireland, Wales, Cornwall and Scotland and included both the Brough of Birsay and the Brough of Deerness, as examples of a monastic type to be seen most clearly at the site of Tintagel in Cornwall. This was elaborated upon in a further paper, in which Papil in Shetland was added to the probable list, and Eynhallow ("holy island") in Orkney was considered as "a small Norse monastery". Other sites were briefly considered in the context of "hermitages", for instance St Ninian's Isle, Shetland, or as "churches of lesser consideration", for instance St Tredwell's chapel on Papa Westray. With the latter, a connection with the Pictish area of activity was accepted, rather than the "Irish west" (Radford 1962b, 165-9). Essentially, Radford held to these views in his paper on "Birsay and the Spread of Christianity to the North", published in 1983, merely amending his interpretation of St Ninian's Isle, by analogy with the Brough of Birsay, from hermitage to monastery (Radford 1983, 18-20).

The site of the Brough of Birsay, now a tidal island, is one that lends itself to such an interpretation and there are a number of individual features which have been cited in support of this. Radford has considered one excavated

feature to be a *leacht* (Radford 1959, 17-18; Radford 1962a, Plate II (b); Radford 1962b, 168-9; Cruden 1965, 25), and he has also emphasised its position within a cemetery of two phases, the latter of which is Norse, and the earlier therefore deduced to be Pictish or "Celtic". This cemetery has been associated by Radford and Stewart Cruden with the earlier features below a small stone church at the centre of the cemetery, and what has been described as a curvilinear enclosure underlying a later rectangular enclosure (Radford 1959; Cruden 1965). It is unfortunate - to say the least - that the previous excavations in this crucially important part of the site are still not published in final form, so that the cemetery features and structural evidence in the immediate vicinity of the chapel can barely be assessed (but see Morris forthcoming a and b for assessment of pre- and post-War excavations). A number of cross-decorated slabs have been found which could also be attributed to this period.

However, we may now question each of these attributions. We might now ask whether the so-called *leacht* may more plausibly represent the remains of a Pictish platform-cairn, as now identified from other sites in Northern Scotland (including Birsay Bay - as discussed above)? And if so, then, again, the recent parallels would suggest that it could well have been surmounted originally by a Pictish symbol-stone. Being placed in the area of the later Christian cemetery, it would then presumably have had particular significance. The simplicity of the designs of the cross-slabs preclude an attribution to the earlier, pre-Norse, rather than the later, Christian Norse, period. It can now be stated that, apart from the unconvincing plan of this enclosure, there are grounds for questioning the attribution of some of the elements making up this "feature" to the pre-Viking period (see Morris 1982b). Equally, the earlier stone foundation is precisely analogous to that found at Deerness which I have argued elsewhere is, despite equivocal dating evidence, best seen in a Christian Norse context (Morris with Emery 1986; Morris 1990); Radford has recently accepted a Norse date for it (Radford 1983, 24 and 31). As at St Ninian's Isle, the 'Celtic' or pre-Norse church and enclosure now has to be regarded as "hypothetical" (see Thomas 1973b, 11-14; 1983, 287-8). This is not to deny the evidence, already alluded to above, for fine metalworking and other craft activities - in the region of a small well to the east of the church (Curle 1982, Ill 5, 16) - as well as demonstrably Pictish or pre-Viking artefacts from several locations on the site, and the various building remains uncovered by John Hunter and myself further away from this later ecclesiastical focus. There can be little doubt that the site as a whole had "special status", but, as Dr John Hunter has said, whether it "derived from political considerations or monastic impetus is...finely balanced according to current evidence" (Hunter 1986, 171). In this writer's opinion, the balance is now firmly tipping towards the political.

I have elsewhere discussed in detail the evidence from other sites in Orkney and Shetland brought forward by Dr Radford (Morris 1990), and have argued that, despite the manifestly important stone shrines and Pictish silver treasure from St Ninian's Isle, and similar shrines at Papil (Thomas 1973a; 1973b; 1983; MacRoberts 1965; Wilson 1969; 1973), the evidence for a monastic establishment at either site is questionable. Similarly, from my own excavations at the Brough of Deerness, I have concluded that there is an absence of firm evidence for such an establishment there at the pre-Norse period (Morris with Emery 1986). Indeed, I would argue that the evidence here, by analogy with other sites in the North Atlantic region, best fits with an explanation in terms of the Christian Norse period. By extension I have, therefore, raised the question as to whether the stone building that Thomas has hypothesised (Thomas 1973b, 11-14; 1983, 287-8) below the later stone chapel (itself of two phases) from St Ninian's Isle could come from a later (i.e. Norse) period? In the light of evidence discussed from the Brough of Deerness, it might be asked whether this is not a more credible explanation of the evidence? It is also far from clear that the treasure from the site was *necessarily* from inside a building. (This does not preclude the possibility of a yet earlier building, perhaps of timber, unrecognised or unrecorded in the excavations of 1958). It would seem to me inescapable that the logic of the argument requires the earlier foundations at the Brough of Birsay to come from the same period; and to be seen perhaps in the context of a private chapel of the Norse Earl. I would argue now that the Early Christian date and 'Celtic' monastic model has become something of a straightjacket.

Having asserted that the direct evidence for the Brough of Birsay as a *monastic* site of the so-called 'Celtic church' in the pre-Viking period is both questionable and, on the basis of parallels elsewhere, perhaps better explained in a later Norse context, I will now turn to the evidence for Western Britain, from where Dr Radford derived his 'model'. I think that we can now assert that the evidence, perhaps from Gateholm in Dyfed, and certainly from Tintagel in Cornwall, is better explained in terms of a secular power-centre rather than an ecclesiastical site. This does not lessen the importance of Birsay, but simply places it into another context - as indeed I think the evidence for Tintagel also shows it to be best explained.

Tintagel and Western Britain

In the paper from 1962 already referred to, the links around northern and western Britain, or "Celtic Britain", were emphasised by Dr Ralegh Radford. Tintagel, Gateholm, the Brough of Deerness and the Brough of Birsay became key sites in the exposition of the theme of "The Celtic Monastery in Britain" (Radford 1962a). Despite criticisms in the 1970s (Burrow 1973), Radford maintained his position over the interpretation of Tintagel (Radford 1935; 1939; 1942; 1956; 1968; 1973; 1975), and was followed in this by leading church archaeologists such as Professor Cramp (Cramp 1976) and Professor Thomas (Thomas 1971a and b, but see Thomas 1982). This is not the place to discuss the historiography of the site of Tintagel, but work in the 1980s by Dark (1985), Thomas and Fowler (1985) and Thomas and others (Thomas 1988a and b; Thomas and Thorpe 1988; Thomas (ed) 1988) has led subsequently to the "Deconstruction of a Monastery" (Thomas 1993). Simultaneously, renewed

Fig. 3.10. Tintagel, Cornwall: aerial photograph (Cornwall Archaeological Unit)

excavations both on the Island and the Churchyard sites in the 1990s have examined several aspects of the new approach to Tintagel and this recent work is beginning to be brought into the public domain via interim reports (Morris, Nowakowski and Thomas 1990; Nowakowski and Thomas 1991; Nowakowski and Thomas 1992; Morris with Emery and others 1991; Morris with Harry, Johnson and others 1993; Morris (ed) 1994; Harry and Morris (eds) 1995) and the first of the final reports on work on the Island is now available (Batey, Sharpe and Thorpe 1993). This is not the place in which to enter into a discusssion of the details of these excavations, which are ongoing, but it can certainly be stated that, for the present, Tintagel no longer provides a monastic 'model' against which other sites such as the Brough of Birsay might be judged. We are beginning in this work to 'flesh out' a new interpretation of the island site as a secular stronghold of the early rulers of Cornwall (Fig. 3.10) but associated with an ecclesiastical focus in the area of the modern Parish Church. We also see it as intimately involved in trade and exchange with the Mediterranean world - as evidenced by imported pottery - and as remaining as a key site of the period, if in a radically different role.

Brief reference has been made above to the reinterpretation by the author of the Brough of Deerness (Morris 1977; Morris with Emery 1986; Morris 1990) and we might also add that the fourth of the major sites brought forward by Radford for his Celtic monastic 'model', Gateholm in Dyfed, no longer appears to fit the requirements. Excavated in 1909 (Cantrill 1910) and 1929 (Lethbridge and David 1930), it shared many features with Tintagel as perceived in the inter-War and post-War years: isolated location, enclosing bank, groupings of rectangular huts. (Fig. 3.11) Work in the 1970s (Davies *et al* 1971) and a recent

Fig. 3.11. Gateholm, Dyfed: plan (A Lane after Davies et al *and Cantrill)*

summary of the evidence (Lane 1988) emphasises the unique nature of the site and the lack of conclusive evidence to link it with a monastic interpretation.

Thus, we might well now raise serious questions about the interpretations based upon older perceptions of the individual layouts of these sites, or comparisons between them, their dating to a "Celtic" context or indeed their attribution as monastic sites, both in the particular and in general. The notion of a "Celtic monastery" in the north and west of Britain has dissolved - at least in respect of the sites upon which Radford's 'model' was founded. However, even if we might substitute "secular" for "monastic" in some or all cases, or possibly even re-date one or more to a later period, all of these quasi-offshore islands, apparently in peripheral locations, would appear to have had a considerable political, economic and cultural significance within contemporary society. Even the least explored of these sites - Gateholm - is remarkable in the scale of the number of individual building foundations to be found upon it (at least 110, if not 130: Davies *et al* 1971; Cantrill 1910), and this is now comparable with the numbers recognised in the re-survey of Tintagel Island after the fire of 1983 on the plateau of the Island (Thomas and Fowler 1985). Similarly, survey at Deerness located more, and more regularly aligned, buildings than had previously been recognised (Morris 1977), and the excavations of the 1970s and 1980s at the Brough of Birsay have uncovered buildings in areas well outside the boundaries of the area in the care of the Secretary of State for Scotland (Morris 1980; 1981; 1982b; Hunter 1983; 1986). Cornish, Welsh and Pictish as these individual sites may have been, in more general terms, they appear to share several common features.

These similarities would incline me to a more general view of society in northern and western Britain in this period which has more similarities than differences. At least one modern historian has suggested that we should use the term "Pictish" to describe all those people north of the Forth-Clyde line from AD 80 onwards, regardless of the various tribal names which have come down to us from the period before AD 297 (Smyth 1984, 44-5). The "Picts" may have seemed distinctive to those who, like the Romans, faced their opposition, but alongside their distinctiveness was a fundamental similarity to their Celtic cousins in other parts of Britain. Although there may have been differences deriving from a differing language base, the adoption of the ogam inscriptions in northern as well as western Britain is one obvious example of this phenomenon. Certainly they shared several elements in a basic cultural assemblage (such as

bone pins, antler combs etc) with a wider northern and western British "cultural orbit", and we might wish to point to a common concern with fine metalworking at places such as Brough of Birsay (Curle 1982), Dunadd in Argyll (Campbell and Lane 1993) and Dinas Powys (Alcock 1963) in South Wales, all nominally high status sites of differing groups of "Celtic" peoples.

In the past, the northern Pictish area has perhaps been neglected, almost marginalised, as attention has concentrated on Strathearn, Fife, Angus and the eastern Grampians and seaboard ("The Province of Mar": cf Simpson 1944), but the archaeological evidence from the Moray Firth area, Birsay in Orkney and St Ninian's Isle in Shetland clearly give strong evidence for a different perception. Within this northern area, Birsay Bay and the 'island' of the Brough within it would seem to have been an important place. Although there are differences in particular details between Birsay and Tintagel (not least in the range of external connections), they did perhaps have a similar role within their contemporary societies within Early Medieval Britain. Both were peninsulas or islands which appear to have functioned as power-centres for their immediate localities and, we presume, for the wider regions. The Brough of Birsay at one extremity of Britain now has a comparable contribution to make to our understanding of this period of protohistory, to that from Tintagel at the other end. It has been my privilege to work on both sites, and if I am now propounding different interpretations to those brought forward by my predecessor, Dr Radford, I am nevertheless only too well aware that all reinterpretation necessarily builds upon the work of those who have gone before and that Dr Radford already saw 'Scotland' in the wider framework of the British Isles in the Early Medieval period.

Dept. of Archaeology
University of Glasgow

Acknowledgements

This paper represents an expanded version of the lecture given in the University of St Andrews in February 1995. I am grateful to Dr Crawford for the invitation to contribute to the Day Conference and to both her and the audience for their tolerance in relation to my illness during the lecture itself; I hope that the printed version is some recompense for the below par performance on the day! The lecture returned in part to a theme which was considered in my O'Donnell

lecture in the University of Wales in 1993. This is currently in process of publication in *Studia Celtica*, and there are inevitably areas of overlap between the two, but the very different context of the two may perhaps provide some justification for the repetition. I am grateful to Dr Colleen Batey for her help with discussion of the content of this text.

References

Alcock, Leslie. 1963. *Dinas Powys. An Iron Age, Dark Age and Early Medieval Settlement in Glamorgan*, Cardiff.

Alcock, Leslie. 1984. A Survey of Pictish Settlement Archaeology, in Friell & Watson (eds) 1984, 7-41.

Anderson, Alan O. (trans). 1922. *Early Sources of Scottish History AD 500-1286*, 2 vols, Edinburgh.

Anderson, Alan O. and Anderson, Marjorie O. (ed & trans). 1961, *Adomnan's Life of Columba*, London

Anderson, Joseph. 1881. *Scotland in Early Christian Times*, The Rhind Lectures in Archaeology, Edinburgh.

Armit, Ian. 1990. Brochs and beyond in the Western Isles, in Armit (ed) 1990, 41-70.

Armit, Ian (ed). 1990. Beyond the Brochs. Changing Perspectives in the Later Iron Age in Atlantic Scotland, Edinburgh.

Ashe, Geoffrey (ed). 1968. *The Quest for Arthur's Britain*, London.

Ashmore, Patrick J. 1980. Low cairns, long cists and symbol stones, *Proc Soc Antiq Scot* 110, 1978-80, 346-355.

Batey, Colleen E. 1989. The Artefactual Assemblage in Morris 1989, Chap 7.

Batey, Colleen E. and Morris, Christopher D. 1983. Part II: The Finds, in Hedges 1983, 85-108.

Batey, Colleen E., Sharpe, Adam and Thorpe, Carl. 1993. Tintagel Castle: archaeological investigations of the Steps are 1989 and 1990, *Cornish Archaeol* 32, 47-66.

Batey, Colleen E., Jesch, Judith and Morris, Christopher D. (eds). 1993. *The Viking Age in Caithness, Orkney and the North Atlantic. Select Papers from the 11th Viking Congress, Kirkwall & Thurso 1989*, Edinburgh.

Bigelow, Gerald F. 1984. Two Kerbed Cairns from Sandwick, Unst, Shetland, in Friell and Watson (eds) 1984, 115-129.

Bigelow, Gerald F. 1985. Sandwick, Unst and Late Norse Shetland Economy, in Smith (ed) 1985, 95-127

Bourke, Cormac. 1980. Early Irish Hand-bells, *J Roy Soc Antiq Ireland* 110, 52-66.

Bourke, Cormac. 1983. The hand-bells of the early Scottish church, *Proc Soc Antiq Scot* 113, 464-468.

Breeze, David J. 1994. The Imperial Legacy - Rome and her Neighbours, in Crawford (ed) 1994, 13-19.

Burrow, Ian C. G. 1973. Tintagel - Some Problems, *Scot Archaeol Forum* 5, 99-103

Campbell, Ewan and Lane, Alan. 1993. Celtic and Germanic Interaction in Dalriada: the 7th-Century Metalworking Site at Dunadd, in Spearman and Higgitt (eds) 1993, 52-63.

Cant, Ronald G. 1983. Introduction, *Orkney Heritage* 2, 7-12.

Cantrill, T. C. 1910. The hut-circles on Gateholm, Pembrokeshire, *Archaeol Cambrensis* LXV, 271-82.

Carter, Stephen P., Haigh, David, Neil, Nigel R. J., and Smith, Beverley. 1984.

Interim report on the structures at Howe, Stromness, Orkney, *Glasgow Archaeol J* 11, 61-73.

Close-Brooks, Joanna. 1980. Excavations in the Dairy Park, Dunrobin, Sutherland, 1977, *Proc Soc Antiq Scot* 110, 1978-80, 328-245.

Close-Brooks, Joanna. 1984. Pictish and other Burials, in Friell and Watson (eds) 1984, 87-114.

Close-Brooks, Joanna. 1989. *Pictish Stones in Dunrobin Castle Museum*, Golspie.

Colgrave, Bertram & Mynors, Richard A. B. (ed & trans). 1981. *Bede's Ecclesiastical History of the English People*, Oxford.

Cramp, Rosemary J. 1976. Monastic Sites, in Wilson (ed) 1976, 201-52.

Crawford, Barbara E. 1983. Birsay and the Early Earls and Bishops of Orkney, *Orkney Heritage* 2, 97-118.

Crawford, Barbara E. 1987. *Scandinavian Scotland*, Scotland in the Early Middle Ages 2, Leicester.

Crawford, Barbara E (ed). 1994. *Scotland in Dark Age Europe*, St John's House Papers No 5, St Andrews.

Crawford, Barbara E (ed). 1995. *Northern Isles Connections. Essays from Orkney and Shetland presented to Per Sveaas Andersen*, Kirkwall.

Crawford, Iain A. 1974. Scot (?), Norseman and Gael, *Scottish Archaeological Forum* 6, 1-16.

Cronyn, Janey M., Morris, Christopher D., and Owen, Olwyn A. 1984. A Decorative Mount from the Brough of Birsay, Orkney: A preliminary Note, *Univs of Durham & Newcastle Upon Tyne Archaeol Reps for 1983* 7, 55-60.

Cruden, Stewart H. 1958. Earl Thorfinn the Mighty and the Brough of Birsay, in Eldjarn (ed) 1958, 156-162.

Cruden, Stewart H. 1965. Excavations at Birsay, Orkney, in Small (ed) 1965, 22-31.

Curle, Cecil L. 1940. The Chronology of the Early Christian monuments of Scotland, *Proc Soc Antiq Scot* 74, 1939-40, 60-116.

Curle, Cecil L. 1974. An engraved lead disc from the Brough of Birsay, Orkney, *Proc Soc Antiq Scot* 105, 1972-4, 301-7.

Curle, Cecil L. 1982. *The Pictish and Norse Finds from the Brough of Birsay 1934-74*. Society of Antiquaries of Scotland Monograph Series 1, Edinburgh

Curle, Cecil L. 1983. The Finds from the Brough of Birsay 1934-1974, *Orkney Heritage* 2, 67-81

Dark, Kenneth R. 1985. The plan and interpretation of Tintagel, *Cambridge Medieval Celtic Stud* 9, 1-18.

Davies, Jeffrey L., Hague, Douglas B. and Hogg, A. H. A. 1971. The hut settlement on Gateholm, Pembrokeshire, *Archaeol Cambrensis* 120, 102-10.

Dumville, David N. 1976. A Note on the Picts in Orkney, *Scot Gaelic Stud* XII, 266.

Edwards, Nancy and Lane, Alan. 1988. *Early Medieval Settlements in Wales AD 400-1000*, Bangor/Cardiff.

Eldjarn, Kristján (ed). *Third Viking Congress, Reykjavik 1956*, Reykjavik.

Farrer, James. 1862. The Knowe of Saverough, *Gentleman's Magazine* 213, 601-4.

Fenton, Alexander and Pálsson, Hermann (eds). *The Northern and Western Isles in the Viking World. Survival, Continuity and Change*, Edinburgh,

Forsyth, Katherine. forthcoming a. The Ogham-Inscribed Spindle Whorl from Buckquoy: Evidence for the Irish Language in pre-Viking Orkney?, *Proc Soc Antiq Scot*.

Forsyth, Katherine. forthcoming b. *The Ogham Inscriptions of Scotland: An Edited Corpus*, unpub Ph. D. thesis, Dept Celtic Lang & Lit, Harvard Univ.

Friell, J. Gerry P. and Watson, W. Graham (eds.) 1984. *Pictish Studies. Settlement, Burial and Art in Dark Age Northern Britain*, BAR Brit Ser 125, Oxford.

Gelling, Peter S. 1984. The Norse Buildings at Skaill, Deerness, Orkney, and their immediate predecessor, in Fenton and Palsson (eds) 1984, 12-39.

Gelling, Peter S. 1985. Excavations at Skaill, Deerness, in Renfrew (ed) 1985, 176-182.

Gourlay, Robert. 1984. A Symbol Stone and Cairn at Watenan, Caithness, in Friell and Watson (eds) 1984, 131-4.

Harden, Donald B. (ed). 1956. *Dark Age Britain. Essays to E. T. Leeds*, London.

Harding, Dennis W and Armit, Ian. 1990. Survey and Excavation in West Lewis, in Armit (ed) 1990, 71-107.

Harry, Rachel C. and Morris, Christopher D. (eds). 1995. *Tintagel Castle Excavations 1994*, English Heritage/Univ of Glasgow.

Hedges, John W. 1983. Trial excavations on Pictish and Viking settlements at Saevar Howe, Birsay, Orkney, *Glasgow Archaeological Journal* 10, 73-124 & Microfiche 40-102

Hedges, John W. 1987. *Bu, Gurness and the Brochs of Orkney*, 3 vols, BAR Brit Ser 163-5, Oxford (with the collaboration of Bernard Bell).

Hedges, John W. and Bell, Bernard. 1980. The Howe. *Current Archaeol* 7, 48-51.

Henderson, Isabel. 1958. The Origin Centre of the Pictish Symbols Stones, *Proc Soc Antiq Scot* XCI, 1957-8, 44-60.

Henderson, Isabel. 1971. North Pictland, in Meldram (ed) 1971, 37-52.

Henderson, Isabel. 1975. Inverness, A Pictish Capital, in Inverness Field Club 1975, 91-103.

Henderson, Isabel. 1990. *The Art and Function of Rosemarkie's Pictish Monuments*, Groam House Lecture, Rosemarkie.

Hunter, John R. 1982. Glass: A Report, in Curle 1982, 46-7.

Hunter, John R. 1983. Recent Excavations on the Brough of Birsay, *Orkney Heritage* 2, 152-170.

Hunter, John R. 1986. *Rescue Excavations on the Brough of Birsay* 1974-82. Society of Antiquaries of Scotland Monograph Series 4, Edinburgh.

Hunter, John R. 1990. Pool, Sanday: A Case Study for the Late Iron Age and Viking Periods, in Armit (ed) 1990, 175-197.

Hunter, John R. and Morris, Christopher D. 1982. Appendix: Excavation of Room 5, Brough of Birsay, Clifftop Settlement, 1973-4, in Curle 1982, 124-138.

Jackson, Kenneth H. 1955. The Pictish Language, in Wainwright (ed) 1955, 129-160.

Inverness Field Club. 1975. *The Hub of the Highlands. The Book of Inverness and District*, Edinburgh.

Jackson, Kenneth H. 1977. Appendix 6. The ogam inscription on the spindle whorl, from Buckquoy, Orkney, in Ritchie 1977, 221-2.

Kaland, Sigrid H. H. 1993. The Settlement of Westness, Rousay, in Batey, Jesch and Morris (eds) 1993, 308-317.

Lamb, Raymond G. 1993. Carolingian Orkney and its transformation, in Batey, Jesch and Morris (eds) 1993, 260-271.

Lamb, Raymond G. 1995. Papil, Picts and Papar, in Crawford (ed) 1995, 9-27.

Lane, Alan. 1988. Gateholm, in Edwards and Lane (eds) 1988, 72-5.

Lethbridge, Thomas C. and David, H. E. 1930. Excavation of a house-site on Gateholm, Pembrokeshire, *Archaeol Cambrensis* LXXV, 366-74.

MacDonald, Aidan D. S. 1977. Old Norse "Papar" Names in N and W Scotland, *Northern Stud* 9, 25-30 [reprinted in *Studies in Celtic Survival*, ed. Lloyd R. Laing, BAR Brit Ser, Oxford, 25-30].

MacGregor, Arthur. 1974. The Broch of Burrian, North Ronaldsay, Orkney, *Proc Soc Antiq Scot* 105 (1972-4), 63-118.

MacRoberts, David. 1965. The ecclesiastical significance of the St Ninian's Isle treasure, in Small (ed) 1965, 224-246.

Mann, John C. 1974. The Northern Frontier after AD 369, *Glasgow Archaeol J* 3, 34-42.

Marwick, Hugh. 1952. *Orkney Farm Names*, Kirkwall.

Maxwell, Gordon. 1987. Settlement in Southern Pictland - A New Overview, in Small (ed) 1987, 31-44.

Meldram, Edward (ed). 1971. *The Dark Ages in the Highlands*, Inverness Field Club.

Morris, Christopher D. 1977. The Brough of Deerness, Orkney: a new survey, *Archaeologia Atlantica* 2, 65-79.

Morris, Christopher D. 1980. Excavations at Birsay 1979, *Northern Stud* 16, 17-28, and *Univs of Durham and Newcastle Upon Tyne Archaeol Reps for 1979* 3, 22-31.

Morris, Christopher D. 1981. Excavations at Birsay, Orkney, 1980. *Univs of Durham & Newcastle Upon Tyne Archaeol Reps for 1980*, 4, 35-40.

Morris, Christopher D. 1982a. The Vikings in the British Isles: some aspects of their settlement and economy, in *The Vikings*, ed. Robert T. Farrell, Chichester, 70-94.

Morris, Christopher D. 1982b. Excavations at Birsay, *Univs of Durham & Newcastle Upon Tyne Archaeol Reps for 1981* 5, 46-53.

Morris, Christopher D. 1983. Excavations around Birsay Bay, Orkney, *Orkney Heritage* 2, 119-151.

Morris, Christopher D. 1985. Viking Orkney, in Renfrew (ed) 1985, 210-242.

Morris, Christopher D. 1989. *The Birsay Bay Project Volume 1. Brough Road Excavations 1976-1982*, University of Durham, Department of Archaeology, Monograph Series 1, Durham.

Morris, Christopher D. 1990. *Church and Monastery in the Far North. An Archaeological Evaluation. Jarrow Lecture 1989*. Jarrow.

Morris, Christopher D. Forthcoming. *Brough of Birsay, Orkney. Excavations 1974-1981.*

Morris, Christopher D. (ed). 1994. *Tintagel Castle Excavations 1993* by Rachel C. Harry and Paul G. Johnson, English Heritage/Univ of Glasgow.

Morris, Christopher D., Nowakowski, Jacqueline and Thomas, A. Charles 1990. Tintagel, Cornwall: the 1990 excavations, *Antiquity* 64, No 245, 843-9.

Morris, Christopher D. with Emery, Norman. 1986. The chapel and enclosure on the Brough of Deerness, Orkney, survey and excavations, 1975-7, *Proc Soc Antiq Scot* 116, 301-374 & fiches 2-4.

Morris, Christopher D. with Emery, Norman. 1991. *Tintagel Castle Excavations 1990,* English Heritage/Univ of Durham.

Morris, Christopher D. with Harry, Rachel C. and Johnson, Paul G. 1993. *Tintagel Castle Excavations 1991,* English Heritage/Univ of Glasgow.

Morris, John (ed & trans). 1980. *Nennius' British History and the Welsh Annals,* Chichester.

Neil, Nigel R. W. 1985. Excavations at Howe, Stromness, in Renfrew (ed) 1985, 205-7.

Nowakowski, Jacqueline and Thomas, A. Charles. 1991. *Tintagel Churchyard Excavations at Tintagel Parish Church, North Cornwall Spring 1990. An Interim report*, Truro.

Nowakowski, Jacqueline and Thomas, A. Charles. 1992. *Grave News from Tintagel. An Illustrated Account of Archaeological Excavations at Tintagel Churchyard, Cornwall 1991*, Truro.

O'Connor, Anne and Clarke, David V. (eds). 1983. *From the Stone Age to the Forty-five. Studies to R.B.K. Stevenson*, Edinburgh.

Palsson, Hermann and Edwards, Paul (trans). 1978. *Orkneyinga Saga. The History of the Earls of Orkney*, London.

Pearce, Susan M. (ed). *The Early Church in Western Britain and Ireland*, BAR Brit Ser 102, Oxford

Petrie, George. 1973. Notice of the Brochs or Round Towers of Orkney, *Archaeol Scot* V, 71-94.

Radford, C. A. Ralegh. 1935. Tintagel: the Castle and Celtic Monastery. Interim report, *Antiq J* XV, 401-19.

Radford, C. A. Ralegh. 1939. *Tintagel Castle*, Official guide, 2nd ed, London.

Radford, C. A. Ralegh. 1942. Tintagel in History and Legend, *J Roy Inst Cornwall* LXXXVI (No 86) = Appendix for 1942, 25-41.

Radford, C. A. Ralegh. 1956. Imported Pottery found at Tintagel, Cornwall, in Harden (ed) 1956, 59-70.

Radford, C. A. Ralegh. 1959. *The Early Christian and Norse Settlements at Birsay.* Official Guide, Edinburgh.

Radford, C. A. Ralegh. 1962a. The Celtic Monastery in Britain, *Archaeologia Cambrensis* CXI, 1-24.

Radford, C. A. Ralegh. 1962b. Art and Architecture: Celtic and Norse, in Wainwright (ed) 1962, 163-187.

Radford, C. A. Ralegh. 1968. Romance and Reality in Cornwall, in Ashe (ed) 1968, 59-77.

Radford, C. A. Ralegh. 1973. Summary and Discussion, *Scot Archaeol Forum* 5, 136-40.

Radford, C. A. Ralegh. 1975. Tintagel, in Radford and Swanton (eds) 1976, 16-24.

Radford, C. A. Ralegh. 1983. Birsay and the Spread of Christianity to the North, *Orkney Heritage* 2, 13-35.

Radford, C. A. Ralegh and Swanton, Michael J. (eds). 1975. *Arthurian Sites in the West*, Exeter.

Renfrew, A. Colin (ed). 1985. *The Prehistory of Orkney BC 4000-1000 AD*. Edinburgh.

Ritchie, Anna. 1972. Painted pebbles in early Scotland, *Proc Soc Antiq Scot* 104 (1971-2), 297-301.

Ritchie, Anna. 1974. Pict and Norseman in Northern Scotland, *Scot Archaeol Forum* 6, 23-36

Ritchie, Anna. 1977. Excavation of Pictish and Viking-age farmsteads at Buckquoy, Orkney, *Proc Soc Antiq Scot* 108, 1976-7, 174-227.

Ritchie, Anna. 1983. Birsay Around AD 800, *Orkney Heritage* 2, 46-66.

Ritchie, Anna. 1985. Orkney in the Pictish Kingdom, in Renfrew (ed) 1985, 183-209.

Ritchie, Anna. 1986. *Brough of Birsay*. Official Guide, Edinburgh.

Ritchie, Anna. 1989. *Picts. An Introduction to the Life of the Picts and the Carved Stones in the Care of the Secretary of State for Scotand*, Edinburgh.

Ritchie, J. N. Graham. 1969. Two New Pictish Symbol Stones from Orkney, *Proc Soc Antiq Scot* 101, 1968-9, 130-3.

Ritchie, J. N. Graham and Fraser, Iain. 1994. *Pictish Symbol Stones. A Handlist 1994*, RCAHMS, Edinburgh.

Royal Commission on the Ancient and Historical Monuments of Scotland (RCAHMS). 1946. *Twelfth Report with an Inventory of the Ancient Monuments of Orkney and Shetland. 3 vols,* Edinburgh, nos 1 & 6, 1-5 & 7.

Simpson, W. Douglas. 1944. *The Province of Mar*, Rhind Lectures in Archaeology 1941, Aberdeen Univ Stud 121, Aberdeen.

Skene, William F. 1867. *Chronicles of the Picts and Scots*, Edinburgh.

Skene, William F. 1876. *Celtic Scotland*, 2 vols, Edinburgh.

Small, Alan, Thomas, A. Charles, Wilson, David M. 1973. *St Ninian's Isle and its Treasure*, Aberdeen Univ Stud 152, Oxford.

Small, Alan (ed). *The Fourth Viking Congress, York, August 1961*, Aberdeen University Studies 149, Edinburgh & London.

Small, Alan (ed). 1987. *The Picts. A New Look at Old Problems*, Dundee.

Smith, Beverley. 1990. New Insights into Later Iron Age Settlement in the North: Howe, in Armit (ed) 1990, 32-40.

Smith, Beverley Ballin (ed). 1994. *Howe. Four Millenia of Orkney Prehistory*, Society of Antiquaries of scotland Monograph Series 9, Edinburgh.

Smith, Brian (ed). 1985. *Shetland Archaeology. New Work in Shetland in the 1970s*, Lerwick.

Smyth, Alfred P. 1984. *Warlords and Holymen. Scotland AD 80-1000*, New History of Scotland 1, London.

Spearman, R. Michael and Higgitt, John. (eds). 1993. *The Age of Migrating*

Ideas. Early Medieval Art in Northern Britain and Ireland, Edinburgh and Stroud.

Sterckx, Claude. 1970. Les jeux de damiers celtiques, *Annales de Bretagne* 77, 597-609.

Sterckx, Claude. 1973a. Les trois Damiers de Buckquoy (Orcades), *Annales de Bretagne* 80, 675-689.

Sterckx, Claude. 1973b. Les jeux de damiers celtiques, *Etudes Celtiques* 13, 733-749.

Taylor, Albert B. (ed). 1938. *The Orkneyinga Saga: a new translation with introduction and notes*, Edinburgh & London.

Thomas, A. Charles. 1971a. *The Early Christian Archaeology of North Britain*, Oxford.

Thomas, A. Charles. 1971b. *Rostat*, *Rosnat* and the early Irish Church, *Eriu* XXII, 100-6.

Thomas, A. Charles. 1973a. *Bede, Archaeology and the Cult of Relics. Jarrow Lecture 1989*, Jarrow.

Thomas, A. Charles. 1973b. Sculptured stones and crosses from St Ninian's Isle and Papil, in Small, Thomas and Wilson 1973, 8-44.

Thomas, A. Charles. 1982. East and West: Tintagel, Mediterranean imports and the Early Insular Church, in Pearce (ed), 17-34.

Thomas, A. Charles. 1983. The Double Shrine'A' from St Ninian's Isle, Shetland, in O'Connor and Clarke (eds) 1983, 285-92.

Thomas, A. Charles. 1988a. Tintagel Castle, *Antiquity* 62, 421-434.

Thomas, A. Charles. 1988b. The Context of Tintagel. A New Model for the Diffusion of Post-Roman Mediterranean Imports, *Cornish Archaeol* 27, 7-24.

Thomas, A. Charles. 1993. *Tintagel. Arthur and Archaeology*, London.

Thomas, A. Charles (ed). 1988. *Tintagel Papers = Cornish Stud* 16 (Special Issue).

Thomas, A. Charles and Fowler, Peter J. 1985. Tintagel: a new syrvey of the 'Island', in *The Royal Commisssion on the Historical Monuments of England Annual Review 1984-5*, 16-21.

Thomas, A. Charles and Thorpe, Carl M. 1988. *Catalogue of all non-Medieval Finds from Tintagel*, Tintagel Project No 2, Inst Cornish Stud and English Heritage, unpub report on file in Truro and London.

Thomson, William P. L. 1987. *History of Orkney*, Edinburgh.

Wainwright, Frederick T. 1962. Picts and Scots, in Wainwright (ed) 1962, 91-116.

Wainwright, Frederick T. (ed). 1955. *The Problem of the Picts*, Edinburgh & London.

Wainwright, Frederick T. (ed). 1962. *The Northern Isles*, Edinburgh & London.

Watkins, Trevor F. 1980. Excavation of a settlement and souterrain at Newmill, near Bankfoot, Perthshire, *Proc Soc Antiq Scot* 110, 1978-80, 165-208.

Watkins, Trevor F. 1984. Where were the Picts? An essay in settlement archaology, in Friell & Watson (eds) 1984, 63-86.

Wilson, David M. 1969. *Reflections on the St Ninian's Isle Treasure*, Jarrow Lecture.

Wilson, David M. 1973. The treasure, in *St Ninian's Isle and its Treasure, Aberdeen Univ Stud* 152, Oxford.

Wilson, David M. (ed). 1976. *The Archaeology of Anglo-Saxon England*, London.

Winterbottom, Michael (ed & trans). 1978. *Gildas. The Ruin of Britain*, Chichester.

Trade in the Dark-Age West: a peripheral activity?

Ewan Campbell

1. Introduction

At the 1993 Day Conference 'Scotland in Dark-Age Europe' (Crawford, 1994), Alan Lane presented some of the basic results of my research into the trade and imports in the Celtic West (Lane 1994), so this paper will be more speculative and wide-ranging in an attempt to assess the importance of trade in the period AD 500-800, and its relative importance to Scotland in relation to the rest of western Britain and Ireland.

The 'peripheral' nature of trade which I wish to re-examine has two aspects: the geographical sense, especially in terms of core/periphery models; and the socio-economic sense, relating to the relative importance of trade in the maintenance of social relations.

My reasons for re-assessing the importance of trade derive from a number of recent articles and books which argue that some archaeologists have overemphasised the importance of long-distance trade, and that most of the demonstrable exchange was of fairly minor economic significance and not instrumental in social change (Mytum 1992; Griffiths 1992; Wooding forthcoming). Wooding in particular puts forward a model of trade by coastal tramping, with ships following random routes, driven by the needs of cargoes and clients they encounter in various ports, (which I would paraphrase as the *Para Handy* model). Another aspect of recent criticism is the suggestion that the scale of the finds is not consistent with regular trade, the numbers of imported pottery vessels being compared unfavourably to those found in some mercantile contexts in the Mediterranean, for example the seventh-century Yassi Ada wreck (Alcock and Alcock 1990, Alcock 1995).

No one doubts the importance of the imports in providing a chronological framework for the region, there being no other independent dating mechanism for most sites in this area; or the fact that they illustrate some sort of long-distance contact and brought some exotic objects to Insular sites, but it is the scale and significance of the activity which is disputed.

I would therefore like very briefly to outline the main groups of imports, describe some important recent findings, and defend my thesis that these are the products of well-established trading systems. I will try to look at how we might assess the importance of the trade; and end with some speculation about the processes involved.

2. Summary of import groups

As an excellent summary is given by Lane (1994; see also Campbell forthcoming a), I will not repeat the details here, but include new information from the important site of Whithorn (Campbell forthcoming b) and discoveries in France (Campbell forthcoming c). The earlier system of importation from the Mediterranean region, consists of a package of wares including amphora, carrying oil, wine and other commodities, along with scarcer fine red tableware. The main phase is associated with sources around the Aegean, and dates to the late fifth and early sixth centuries, with a much smaller component from Carthage area, datable to the second quarter of the sixth century. This was directed trade focused on tin and lead/silver producing areas of south-west Britain.

The later Continental system can now be seen to also have two phases. The earlier consists of fine black tableware (D ware), from south-west France in the middle half of the sixth century, and recently identified glass from the same area (Campbell forthcoming c). Later, the volume of goods increased with more glass, now accompanied by small storage vessels and minor tableware in a coarse fabric (E ware), again deriving from western France, but in the later sixth, with a *floruit* in the early seventh century and continuing to the end of the seventh. As with the earlier system, the pottery containers carried goods rather than being trade items in their own right, as Thomas has suggested in the past. Scientific analysis has shown traces of non-native red dyestuffs (Dyer's Madder) on some vessels, and I have suggested on the basis of contemporary documentary evidence that other commodities such as honey, fruits, nuts and spices may have been carried. Indeed, seeds of non-native plants such as the spice coriander and the herb dill have been found in recent excavations at Buston crannog (Holden 1995), a site with E ware which has also produced traces of madder dye. However, the bulk of any cargo was probably salt and wine from the west of France. The insular distribution lies further north than the Mediterranean imports, around the Irish Sea and western Scotland.

3. Trade or not?

The criticisms outlined in the introduction lead me to reassert my belief that the distribution patterns shown by the imports are the result of sustained, regular, directed trade, (in other words mercantile trade), rather than one of the alternative options, such as the tramping model of Wooding. Other minimalist explanations include that of Charles Thomas (1990), who has suggested that most of the Mediterranean imports could be the result of one, or very few, voyages of merchant entrepreneurs. This can be described as the *Columbus* model , where a merchant adventurer sets out into the unknown in the hope of discovering unknown riches. Another view is that the imports could be the chance keepsakes of returning travellers, such as pilgrims, tourists or mercenaries. Professor Vera Evison (1979) has suggested this explanation for the sixth and seventh century Anglo-Saxon pottery imports to Kent, in what might be called the *duty-free bottle* model.

As far as the Mediterranean imports are concerned the date of the wares can now be ascertained quite closely from work at Carthage and elsewhere (Fulford & Peacock 1984). The minimum period covered by the different tableware forms found in Britain is a generation, with some vessels that can be dated to around AD 500 and others to AD 525/35, but the likely span is more, probably 50 years from 500-550. This spread of dates in itself shows continuing contact. More convincing evidence comes from the study of the Mediterranean patterns of trade, which shows that Phocaean Red Slipware was restricted to the eastern Mediterranean except in the period AD 475-550, when its range expands dramatically with exports to Italy, Spain and Portugal (Hayes 1974, maps 31-4). The British distribution is quite clearly an extension of this trade and of the same character, with the same package of wares, and should date over the same range of time. Furthermore, it is difficult to see why a round voyage of 10,000 km from Byzantium should be undertaken on the off-chance that some significant trade goods would be available on arrival in Britain. A cargo load of tin, taking the Yassi Ada ship as a model (Bass & van Doornick 1984), would be around 40 tons. This would represent a large commitment of effort and time to mine and refine on the part of the British, an effort unlikely to be undertaken without a guarantee that the Byzantine merchants would appear, even if only once a year. Of course the same applies in reverse to the merchants. Although it was short-lived, I would suggest this was a true trading venture, though whether it was undertaken by entrepreneurial merchants in a period of lax imperial control (Fulford 1989), or by imperial procurators of supplies, could be debated.

Turning to the Continental imports, the E ware vessels are so similar in form and fabric that they must be all from a set of related kilns from a restricted area, and the same applies to the distinctive decorated glass which differs from that of Northern France (Fig. 4.3) (Campbell forthcoming c). There were many types of pottery in production in Francia at this period which would be reflected in the finds if Insular traders were visiting the Continent, or if a variety of traders were coming to Insular areas. For comparison, at Middle Saxon *Hamwic* some ninety different varieties of imported pottery are recorded, many provenanced to various parts of north-western France and Belgium (Timby 1988). New evidence from Whithorn, the first western site to have a good stratified sequence of deposits, shows the imported pottery continuing through most of 18 sub-phases deposited between AD 500 and 700, which must indicate that regular shipments of Mediterranean and Continental wares were arriving (Campbell forthcoming b). Again it seems clear that foreign merchants from one particular region were deliberately targeting western Insular areas over a period of some 100-150 years, suggesting mercantile trade aimed at satisfying a particular need for commodities available in these areas. The nature of these commodities is unknown, though they must have been organic, as surviving artefacts of Insular origin are almost unknown in France at this period. Suggestions have included slaves, leather goods, furs, and perhaps even cereals.

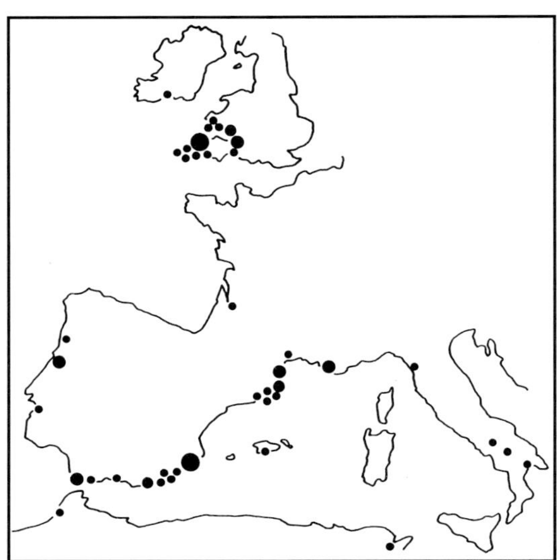

Fig. 4.1. Distribution of Phocaean Red Slipware in western Europe. Size of symbol is proportional to number of vessels.

One argument against the distribution being the

result of trade is the scale of the finds. The total number of vessels so far known is relatively small though it is growing rapidly from the current tally of 300 Mediterranean and 500 Continental. However, it is not suggested that in either system the main item of trade was the pottery, which may have been incidental to the main cargo of perishable goods. In many known Mediterranean wrecks pottery is only a minor element of mixed cargoes (Parker 1984). Even so, the British numbers compare well with those from western Mediterranean sites (Fig. 4.1). It is also perhaps instructive to look at another example of imported pottery on western sites, namely the thirteenth- and fourteenth-century Saintonge ware from the same region of south-west France as the sixth/seventh century imports, and itself certainly the product of mercantile trade. The total numbers of vessels and sites until recently was similar to that of E ware, but John Allan has estimated, using later Exeter Port Books statistics, that millions of Saintonge pots may have been imported, and that urban excavations may be revealing only one thousandth of the imported amount (Allan 1983). While the figures cannot be taken at face value, this does illustrate that small numbers of pots may be the only visible residue of a much more significant trading system.

4. Socio-economic context of the import sites

How can we assess the socio-economic importance of this trade? The archaeologist has only two options, to analyse where and in what context the imports are found, and to look at patterns over time.

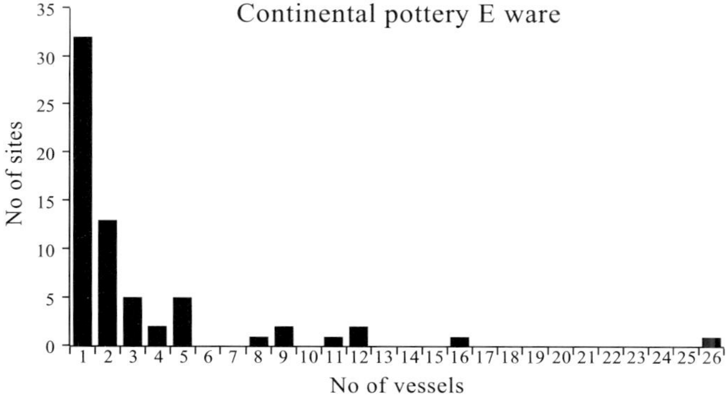

Fig. 4.2. Relative frequency of imported E ware on Insular sites, shown by number of vessels per site. Dunadd is the site with most vessels.

By analysing the number of vessels found on sites a hierarchy is immediately apparent: a few have many vessels, most have one or two, many more have none (Fig. 4.2). The use of minimum numbers of vessels is a widely accepted statistical technique for comparing medieval and Roman pottery assemblages from different sites (the number of sherds is of no significance, cf. Alcock 1995, 141). It is possible to show that the sites with many vessels acted as centres of importation, with redistribution to lower status sites in their hinterland. In Ireland it is even possible in places to show political control over redistribution (Campbell 1991). If the characteristics of the major sites are examined it can be seen that there are three types of site: defended centres, undefended centres, and trading places (Ibid). It is the high status defended centres I want to look at in detail. These have a set of characteristics which distinguish them from the other types of site (Table 4.1). They show control of extensive resources and labour: for example at Cadbury Castle, Somerset, 1 km of timber-laced rampart was constructed. Weapons, including swords characteristic of warrior aristocrats, are found. Precious metals, which Irish law tracts suggest were the prerogative of the upper levels of society, are found alongside large-scale production of personal jewellery. In particular, these often consist of ornate brooches which Nieke (1992) has shown to have symbolic importance as a means of displaying and controlling rank. Finally, several have documentary evidence for royal status. Given the gaps in the archaeological record, this is an impressive package of shared characteristics, which might lead one to suggest that the sites without documentary evidence for royal status may indeed have been royal.

I am not the first to put forward an explanation of the function of these central defended sites in terms of potentates accumulating surplus, using it to controlling access to exotic goods, enhancing the power of an elite group and reinforcing social relationships through gift-giving of scarce resources. But are the imports central to this? Were they one of many such social controls, or the main catalyst to the development of concentration of power, or the main support for its maintenance? There clearly is a relationship between the power centres and the imports, but only by means of changes over time can we tell whether they were important, by looking at what happens when the trade stops.

As far as the Mediterranean system is concerned, by 550 all the main fortified centres had been abandoned, and settlement in Cornwall became a pattern of dispersed and undefended enclosures, at least by the seventh century (Preston-Jones and Rose, 1986). This seems to indicate the collapse of central power structures. Some have seen this in terms of Anglo-Saxon advance, with the Battle of Dyrham in 577 as a key factor. Even without questioning the

Table 4.1: Characteristics of major import sites

Site	imports	defended	gold/ silver	brooch/ production	glass-working	weapons	royal
Defended sites							
Dunadd	Cont.	yes	yes	yes	yes	yes	yes
Mote of Mark	Cont.	yes	yes	yes			
Dumbarton	Cont. Med.	yes	yes			yes	yes
Clogher	Cont. Med	yes	yes	yes	yes		yes
Lagore	Cont.	yes	yes	yes	yes	yes	yes
Garranes	Cont. Med.	yes		yes			yes
Garryduff	Cont.	yes	yes	yes	yes	yes	
Dinas Powys	Cont. Med.	yes	yes	yes	yes	yes	
Undefended sites							
Longbury	Cont. Med.	no	yes	yes			
Whithorn	Cont. Med.	no	yes		yes		
South-west Britain							
Cadbury Congresbury	Med.	yes	yes	yes			
Cadbury Castle	Med.	yes					
Tintagel	Med.	yes					
Trading sites							
Samson, Scilly	Cont. Med.	no					
Dalkey Island	Cont. Med.	no					

Cont.: Continental Med.: Mediterranean

significance of the Chronicle entry relating to Dyrham (which has been done), this is stretching the evidence for Cadbury Castle and Cadbury Congresbury, as there is little evidence of Saxon settlement before the seventh century (Rahtz & Watts 1989), and it is patently absurd for Tintagel which lies in an area not settled by Saxons until the tenth century. I suggest that the withdrawal of the Mediterranean market for metals caused social collapse, as the economic power base of the rulers was based on a single commodity (like the cash crops of some present third world countries) and that the later Saxon advance was into this power vacuum.

The picture regarding the Continental import system is more complicated. After 700 some power centres disappear, notably Clogher, Dinas Powys, Longbury and Garranes. Some, such as Whithorn and the Mote of Mark, come into the Anglo-Saxon orbit and are removed from the Celtic culture province. But some such as Dumbarton, Lagore and Garryduff continue, and Dunadd even expands in the eighth century. This suggests that in contrast to the south-western sites, some of these sites may have had a broader economic base, with access to other forms of wealth which was not dependent solely on external markets, thus enabling their rulers to replace the missing exotica and continue social control using other mechanisms or goods.

There are some clues to what might have been going on in the north in the later sixth century. In Ireland there is an explosion in new sites, of two main types, ringforts and crannogs, the latter of which needed large resources of timber and labour to build. Whatever the cause, and Mytum (1992) has suggested the introduction of new technologies such as coulter ploughs and water-driven horizontal mills, there seems to have been increased production, with surplus directed into building and also fine metalwork. This surplus may have been the stimulus for the development of the new power centres, disturbing the economic steady-state of a kin-based

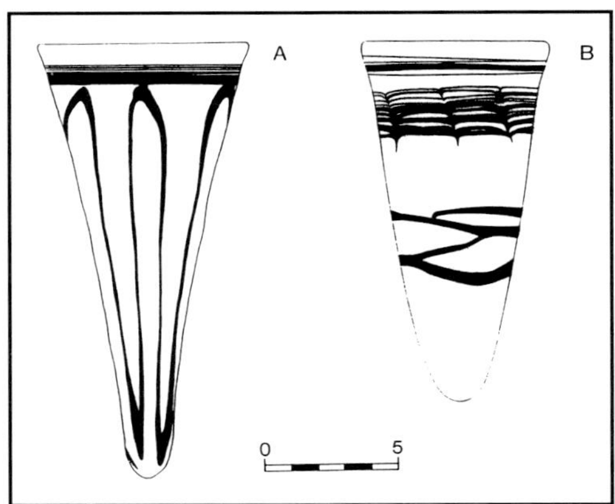

Fig. 4.3. Reconstruction of glass vessels with opaque white trailed decoration from Dinas Powys (left) and Whithorn Priory (right).

system where small surpluses were absorbed and redistributed between lords and clients. The timely appearance of foreign merchants may have served as a useful outlet for the new wealth while increasing the power of the contemporary kings. The next few centuries saw a gradual agglomeration of power into larger political units in Ireland, though the lack of dynastic succession made it very difficult for power to be inherited in a stable way. The seventh century also saw the rise of the influence of the Church and an increasing involvement in secular politics. The Church was a prime consumer of surplus, both human and material, as the gifts given to it by the wealthy, unlike in secular society, did not have to be reciprocated, as the reward was postponed to the afterlife. In return rulers may have had their power legitimised by the Church. We can see this process at work in Adomnan's account of the relations between Aidan and Columba. When the Continental trading system decreases in the later seventh century, some of the surplus, which had been in effect siphoned off to the Continent, was probably invested in spiritual returns with the Church, and I would suggest that this accounts for the huge changes between 600 and 700 in church art, sculpture and metalwork, although undoubtedly some surplus went into personal secular ostentation.

5. Wider aspects

If we look again at the hierarchy of import sites some interesting figures appear, with a gradual concentration of imports further north towards Scotland as we move from the sixth to seventh centuries. This is illustrated if we look at the five most important import sites, in terms of vessel numbers, in successive periods (Table 4.2). In purely geographical terms this is difficult to explain as one would expect the sites closer to the core economic region to have the larger import assemblages. It suggests that there came to be greater rewards in the

Table 4.2: top five sites in terms of imported vessel numbers

500-550	525-600	575-650
Tintagel	Whithorn	Dunadd
Whithorn	Cadbury Congresbury	Whithorn
Cadbury Congresbury	Dinas Powys	Dinas Powys
Dinas Powys	Longbury Bank	Samson
Cadbury Castle	Mote of Mark	Mote of Mark

north for the Frankish merchants by the seventh century. As other economic factors presumably remained constant over the insular regions, this could indicate that there was greater political centralisation of resources in Scotland compared to Ireland and Wales, where as I have said there was considerable political fragmentation. Whether there was any diplomatic dimension to this trade in terms of conscious contact between the Merovingian and Dalriadic dynasties is impossible to say, though the route was there and could have been utilised.

If we compare the economic development of the sixth/seventh century Celtic West and Anglo-Saxon England, the West has early examples of long-distance trade and craft specialisation, but lacks further development towards a true market economy, with no indigenous coins, markets, merchants, or towns before the Scandinavian and Anglo-Norman incursions. Trade seems to be directly controlled by royalty, unlike in England, where the *wics* are distanced from the royal sites and under control of royal reeves. In England trading places appear around 700 with the development of *Hamwic,* and although others have been claimed to develop in the seventh century there is as yet no substantial evidence. The establishment of *Hamwic* could perhaps have siphoned off trade from the western seaways, as it would not have been worth the effort of travelling to western Scotland when there was a ready and larger market just across the Channel.

Conclusion

Trade in the West was indeed peripheral in the geographic sense, both in the Mediterranean and Continental phases, with Insular sites merely reacting to developments in core areas over which they had no control. It is hoped that this paper has shown that trade was significant at the socio-economic level, however, and may have had considerable influence over social development. As far as Scotland in Britain is concerned, there are signs that the northern kingdoms were economically more advanced and integrated by 700 than others further south, something which the existence of *Senchus Fer nAlban* itself suggests. This may even have been a contributing factor to the early development of the unified Scottish dynastic state in the ninth century. (Broun 1994).

Department of Archaeology
University of Glasgow

Acknowledgements

I would like to thank Anne Crone (AOC Edinburgh) for the information on plant remains from Buston crannog.

References

Alcock, L & Alcock, E A 1990 "Reconnaissance excavations on Early Historic fortifications and other royal sites in Scotland, 1974-84: 4, Excavations at Alt Clut, Clyde Rock, Strathclyde", 1974-5', *Proc. Soc. Antiq. Scot.* 120, 95-149

Alcock, L 1995 *Cadbury Castle, Somerset: The early medieval archaeology* (Cardiff)

Allan, J. 1983 "Some post-medieval documentary evidence for the trade in ceramics", *in* Davey, P & Hodges, R (eds) *Ceramics and trade*, Sheffield, 37-45

Bass, G.F. & van Doornick, F.H. 1982 *Yassi Ada, a seventh-century Byzantine shipwreck* (Texas)

Broun, D 1994 "The origin of Scottish identity in its European context", in Crawford 1994, 21-31

Campbell, E 1991 *Imported goods in the early medieval Celtic West: with special reference to Dinas Powys*, (Unpublished PhD thesis, University of Wales, College of Cardiff).

Campbell, E forthcoming a "The archaeological evidence for contacts: imports, trade and economy in Celtic Britain AD 400-800", *in* Dark, K R (ed), *External contacts and the economy of Late Roman and Post-Roman Britain* (Woodbridge)

Campbell forthcoming b "Imported pottery and glass from Whithorn" in Hill, P *Excavations at Whithorn Priory*

Campbell, E forthcoming c "A review of glass vessels in western Britain and Ireland AD 400-800" *in* Price J (ed) *Glass in Britain, AD 350-800* (London)

Crawford, B E (ed) 1994 *Scotland in Dark Age Europe* (St Andrews)

Evison, V I 1979 *A corpus of wheel-thrown pottery in Anglo-Saxon graves* (London)

Fulford, M.G. & Peacock, D.P.S. 1984 *Excavations at Carthage: the British mission. Vol. 1(2) The Avenue du President Habib Bourguiba, Salammbo: the pottery and other ceramic objects from the site* (Sheffield)

Fulford, M G 1989 "Byzantium and Britain: a Mediterranean perspective on post-Roman Mediterranean imports in western Britain and Ireland", *Medieval Archaeol.* 33, 1-6

Griffiths, D 1992 "The coastal trading ports of the Irish Sea", in Graham-Campbell, J (ed) *Viking Treasures from the North-West,* Liverpool, 63-72

Hayes, J W 1972 *Late Roman pottery* (London)

Holden, T 1995 "The waterlogged plant remains from Buston crannog", (unpublished AOC report, Edinburgh)

Lane, A 1994 "Trade, gifts, and cultural exchange in Dark-Age Western Scotland", in Crawford 1994, 103-115

Mytum, H 1992 *The origins of Early Christian Ireland* (London)

Nieke, M R 1993 "Penannular and related brooches:secular ornament or symbol in action?", in Higget, J. & Spearman, M.J. (eds) *The Age of Migrating Ideas. Early Medieval Art in Northern Britain and Ireland*, Edinburgh, 128-134

Parker, A J 1984 "Shipwrecks and trade in the Mediterranean", *Archaeol. Review Cambridge* 3, 99-114

Preston-Jones, A & Rose, P 1986 "Medieval Cornwall", *Cornish Archaeol.* 25, 135-185

Rahtz, P.& Watts, L. 1989 "Pagans Hill revisited", *Archaeol. J.* 146, 330-371

Thomas, C. 1990 "'Gallici nautae de Galliarum provinciis' - A sixth/seventh trade with Gaul, reconsidered", *Medieval Archaeol.* 34, 1-26

Timby, J.R. 1988 "The Middle Saxon pottery", *in* Andrews, P. (ed), *Southampton finds, volume 1; the coins and pottery from Hamwic, Southampton* London,73-124

Wooding, J forthcoming *Communication and commerce along the western sealanes AD 400-800* Oxford

Place-names and the Early Church in Eastern Scotland

Simon Taylor

There is a rich seam of ecclesiastical place-names throughout Scotland, which manifests itself in elements such as *annaid, cill, dìseart, *eglēs, tearmann and kirk* (1). We are fortunate in that many of them have been subjected to careful analyses by a host of scholars, such as Geoffrey Barrow, Aidan MacDonald, John MacQueen, W.F.H. Nicolaisen, W.J. Watson and most recently Thomas Clancy (2). Nevertheless, we are still far from exhausting this seam, and in this paper I want to try to howk out a little more from it. I intend to concentrate on two elements in particular. One is the 'weel-kent' Gaelic element *cill* 'church'; the other is the element *both*. This is equally 'weel-kent', but in a pastoral-transhumant context rather than in an ecclesiastical one, since it is the Gaelic word for 'hut, sheiling', or 'bothy'.

I have just completed a PhD on the settlement- and parish-names of Fife (Taylor, 1995). It did not at first surprise me to note that the most frequently occurring element in Fife parish-names was *cill*: Fettykil (the old name for Leslie parish), Kilconquhar, Kilgour (the old name for Falkland parish), Kilmany, Kilrennie, Kinglassie and Methil (3). It did not surprise me because *cill* is by far the most common element in Scottish parish-names, to be found in over 100 of them; while in Ireland it is even more frequent. However, Nicolaisen's distribution map of place-names containing this element throughout Scotland as a whole (for which see Fig. 5.1) clearly showed that Fife was in fact exceptional, since it includes one of only two clusters of *cill*-names which reach the North Sea. The other is in Easter Ross and east Sutherland.

The next step was to verify this distribution in eastern Scotland. The provisional results can be seen on Fig. 5.2. Although not fundamentally different from Fig. 5.1, several points should be noted:

1. In East Fife there are an additional six *cill*-names, which brings the total tally to eleven (see Appendix 2.1).

2. The three dots in south-east Perthshire disappear, leaving the east Fife cluster even more isolated.

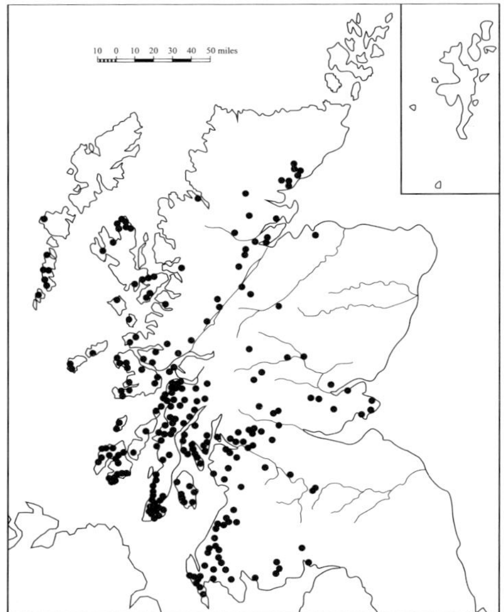

Fig. 5.1. Map of place-names containing cill (Nicolaisen, 1976)

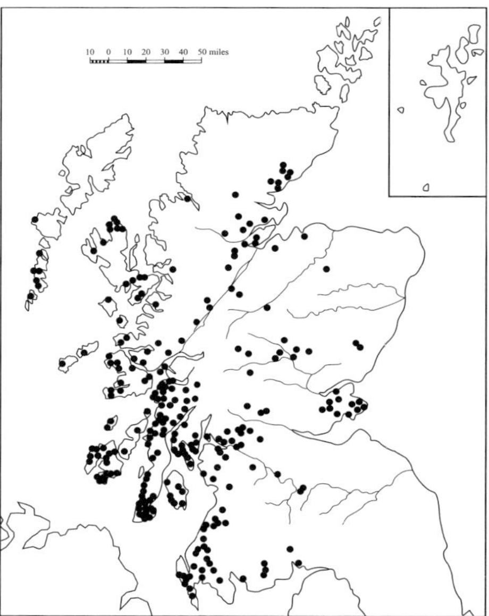

Fig. 5.2. Amended map of place-names containing cill (S. Taylor)

3. The two dots near Logierait on the Tay in Atholl have multiplied to five.

4. Angus is no longer a totally *cill*-free zone, with two examples beside Brechin (4).

Fig. 5.2 shows only those places which contain *cill* beyond reasonable doubt. It is important to stress this point, since *cill* is a notoriously difficult element to identify. It is often confused with Gaelic *coille* 'wood', with *cinn* 'at the end of', and sometimes also with *cùil* 'corner, nook'; or *cùl* 'back'. For example, not only can *cill* end up as *cinn*, as in Kinglassie FIF, but *cinn* can end up as *cill*. A good, if untypical, example of this change, is one that took place when Gaelic was still the main language of east Fife: the Gaelic name for St Andrews is *Cill Rìmhinn,* earlier **Cill Rìgh Mhonaidh,* anglicised as Kilrymonth, and meaning 'church of the royal hill'. It first appears as such in the early twelfth century (e.g. *St A. Lib.* 124). If, as is the case for 99% of Scottish place-names, we had no record of this name prior to 1100, we would certainly have classed it, too, as a *cill*-name. Exceptionally, there are earlier forms going back to the eighth century, and from these it is clear that it was originally **Cinn ríg monaid*, 'at the end of the royal hill'.

Yet another element which often appears as *Kil-* in place-names is the Scots word *kiln*. It is, however, easier to spot, since the second element is also Scots, and the stress pattern is usually different, falling on the first syllable. It is found in such combinations as Kilburn, Kilflat, Kilknowe and Kilfield.

If there were added to Fig. 5.2 doubtful *cill*-names, then the only significant change would be in Aberdeenshire, where there is a handful of problematic names such as Kennethmont (parish), Kilblean (Meldrum parish) and Kinbattock (the old name of Towie parish). But the very rarity of this element in the North-East is itself an argument against these problematic names containing *cill.*

I want now to home in on Fife, or rather east central Scotland. In contrast to east Fife, there is a remarkable dearth of *cill*-names throughout west Fife, Kinross-shire and Clackmannanshire, in short throughout most of the region or province which was known as Fothrif, and which gave its name to one of the deaneries of St Andrews (5). It is therefore of particular significance that in this area two medieval parishes contain the element *both*. These are Tullibole KNR, formerly FIF, and Tullibody CLA. Also there was a chapel of Bath, earlier

Both, near Culross FIF, formerly a detached part of PER; while on the carse lands opposite there was the old parish of Bothkennar in STL. (For more details of all these names, see Appendix 1.) Another striking feature about the three names benorth the Forth is that they all had links with Culross, either proprietorial, with the Cistercian abbey there, or with events in the *Life* of St Serf, whose centre was of course at Culross.

This is not the only part of Scotland where *both* occurs in an ecclesiastical context. Taking parish-names first: in what had once been the northern part of the kingdom of Strathclyde, or neighbouring Brittonic-speaking territory, there are four parishes which contain this element, for which see Appendix 1.1.

North of the Forth, in Pictish territory, there are at least seven medieval parishes with this element. These are also listed in Appendix 1.2, and their distribution is shown on Fig. 5.3. A glance at these lists shows just how well disguised some of these *both*-elements are. This goes some way towards explaining why they have hitherto eluded comment.

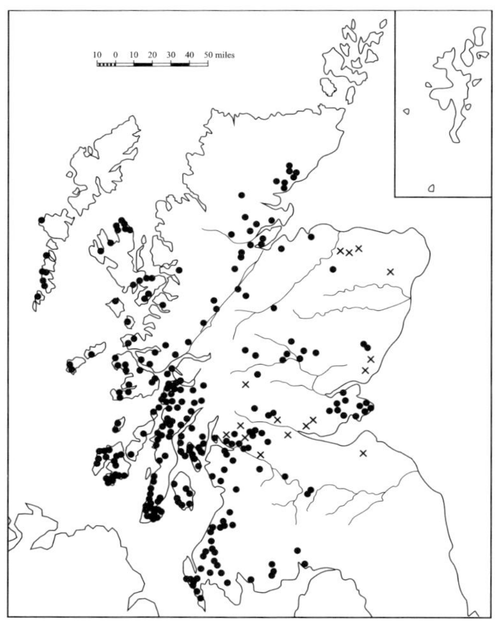

• Name containing *cill*
× Name containing *both* (with religious connotations)

Fig. 5.3 Map of place-names containing cill and both (with religious associations) (S. Taylor)

Included in Appendix 1.2 are three *both*-names which deserve to be mentioned in this discussion, but which do not fit into either of the above categories. Two are medieval parishes lying outwith Strathclyde, Lennox and Pictland: these are Bothan ELO, now the parish of Yester; and Bothkennar STL, which has already been alluded to. As it lies just south of the Forth, opposite Kincardine by Culross, it may

be seen as an outlier of the cluster of ecclesiastical *both*-names on the other side of the river. It contains a female personal name, Cainer, borne by at least two early Irish saints, found also in the parish-name Kirkinner WIG (see Watson, 1926, 166, 275 and 429).

The third such name is the now obsolete Shambothy, 'the place of the old *both*'. This lay beside Clackmannan CLA. It has no specifically religious connotations, but it was the *caput* of a medieval barony, an unusual role for an auld sheiling!

Both also occurs at least three times north of the Forth in conjunction with early chapel-sites, for which see also Appendix 1.3.

Two ecclesiastical *both*-names are linked with a St Ernóc, a diminutive of Ernéne. One, combined with the second person singular possessive pronoun *do*, is the parish of Baldernock STL (see Appendix 1.1); the other, combined with the first person possessive pronoun *mo*, is *Bothmernock ANG. This gives a new twist to the fact that a parish bearing his name, the parish of Marnoch BNF, lies only a few miles east of the remarkable cluster of *both*-parishes in BNF and ABD (Boharm, Botarie and Botriphnie).

The most famous of the many saints called Ernéne or Ernóc was Ernéne mac Cresene, a younger contemporary of Columba, described by Adomnán as famous among all the churches of Ireland, and very widely known (Anderson, 1961, §15b). But as Watson suggests, there might well have been a Scottish saint of that name not recorded by Irish writers (Watson, 1926, 292).

* * * *

The Welsh cognate *bod* means simply 'dwelling, residence', and is mainly found in place-names in north-west Wales. I have counted 24 in all, about one third of which contain personal names. Five of these are parishes (listed in Appendix 1.4), with at least two containing the name of the saint to whom the parish church is dedicated (Bodedern and Bodwrog, both in Anglesey).

Bod is also found unevenly distributed throughout Cornwall. Oliver Padel has counted about 230 *Bod*-names, and concludes that it seems to have meant a dwelling more humble than *tre*, the standard word for a farmstead. He does not note any religious context (Padel, 1985, *s.v.*).

In Old and Middle Irish, according to the Royal Irish Academy's *Dictionary of the Irish Language* (Dublin 1913-), *both* meant 'hut, bothy' or 'cabin', and according to Joyce, 1869, 303-5, it occurs as such in many Irish place-names. I have, however, counted five parishes with this element (for which see Appendix 1.5), one of which, Badoney in County Tyrone, was allegedly founded by Patrick and contains as its second element *domhnach*, a very early word for a church which seems to have fallen out of use by the late seventh century (see Flanagan, 1982, 70-71). In addition there are two or three *both*-names which are attached to saints' names or chapel sites.

So, although in both Wales and Ireland there is sporadic evidence for the religious use of *both*, central and eastern Scotland does seem to have developed this aspect of it more fully than anywhere else in the British Isles.

In Fife and Fothrif, therefore, there are two mutually exclusive clusters of names containing religious elements, with *cill* in the east and *both* in the west (see Fig. 5.3). I now want to develop a tentative hypothesis which will attempt to account for two things: firstly these mutually exclusive clusters; and secondly the fact that the *cill*-cluster in Fife is one of only two along the whole east coast of Scotland.

With respect to east Fife names containing *cill*, it would appear that they were radiating out from some important early church establishment, with Scottish or Irish connections and high political standing. The most obvious candidate for such an establishment was Kinrimonth (*Cinnrígmonaid*), later St Andrews.

In 747 the Annals of Ulster record the death of Tuathalán abbot of *Cinrighmonai*. The abbot's Irish name, and the fact that part of the place-name is Irish, point to a strong link either with Ireland or Dál Riata. Marjorie Anderson suggests that the evidence, slight as it is, indicates a Bangor provenance for this entry (Anderson, 1974, 2). The place must have had a Pictish name, and, since the third element *monadh* is not an Irish word (see Watson, 1926, 391 ff), I would posit a form such as **Pennrígmonad.* That Kinrimonth was an important early secular centre is clear even from the name. There are very few early place-names in Scotland which certainly contain the word for 'king'. There is enough evidence from various sources for general agreement that Kinrimonth was also an important early ecclesiastical centre. It stood under the special patronage of the Pictish kings on account of its alleged possession of relics of the apostle Andrew. Opinions are divided as to which king was responsible for Kinrimonth's elevation of religious status, but whoever it was, there was certainly a monastery here in the mid eighth century important enough for the death of its head to be noted in the Irish annals (see Taylor, 1995, 9 ff).

As far as the creation of *cill*-names in Fife is concerned, we are also looking at a period well before the widespread Gaelicisation of eastern Scotland in the ninth century. The general absence of *cill*-names in Angus and the North-East must mean that *cill* had ceased to be a productive place-name element in the east by the time the Scots settled Pictland to any significant extent. *Cill* is therefore the earliest dateable Gaelic place-name element we have from eastern Scotland, and must date to a period before about 800 (Nicolaisen, 1976, 142-4).

Another way of assessing not only the date, but also the wider historical framework of our *cill*-names is to look at the saints commemorated in them (see Appendix 2). I assume that Ethernan is contained in Kilrenny (*Kilrethni c.*1170) in some mangled or hypocoristic form, since he was obviously an important figure in the area. Kilrenny is a coastal parish, and directly offshore lies the Isle of May, with Ethernan as its patron saint. The name, incidentally, would seem to have been preserved in the place-name Aithernie in Scoonie parish by Leven, further down the coast; while in the old kirkyard of Scoonie itself a Class II Pictish stone was found with an ogham inscription which reads 'Eddarrnonn' (*ECMS* vol.2, 347). The Irish Annals tell us that Itharnan and Corindu died amongst the Picts in 669, but we have no way of knowing whether this was the same person as the Fife saint (*ES* i 180).

Kilminning lies on the coast just east of Crail. The saint commemorated in the name may have been Móinenn of Clonfert, who died in the 570s (see Watson, 1926, 294-5 and 328-9). Whoever he was, his cult persisted along the coast of the East Neuk of Fife for many hundreds of years, and the important fourteenth-century royal foundation at Inverie was dedicated to him. The place later became known as Inverie of St Monan, and is now known simply as St Monance, locally St Minnans.

Of particular relevance to this discussion is the presence of a St Móinenn amidst the other east coast cluster of *cill*-names in Easter Ross. From medieval and early modern documentation we know that there was a chapel of St Monan somewhere near Rosemarkie (MacDowall, 1963, 12). This is a small but significant link between these two areas.

The most noteworthy saint amongst the Fife *cill*-names is that of Duncan, or Dúnchad. This is not because he was such a well-known saint, but because he is commemorated twice, which must be significant. Who was he? There is only one saint of this name mentioned in the early Irish Calendars. He is Dúnchad abbot of Iona, relative of Adomnán, who died 717, and under whose auspices Roman usages were introduced into that abbey (*ES* i 217).

Dúnchad may be the key to our understanding of this *cill*-cluster in east Fife. He lived at a time when controversy was rife in the Scottish and Pictish churches. It was a time when the Pictish king Naiton (or Nechtan) was consciously turning his back on the conservative Columban church, even expelling them from his kingdom, and was looking elsewhere, for example to Northumbria, for guidance in the new ways.

The hypothetical historical frame-work which I would like to propose to account for the distribution of *cill* and *both* in Fife and the adjacent area to the west, as shown on Fig. 5.3, is this: the *cill*-names in east Fife were created in the early eighth century, spreading out from an Irish or Dál Riatan monastic centre under royal patronage at Kinrimonth, which was consciously modernising and promoting Roman usages in accordance with the wishes of King Naiton. We know from Bede that Naiton had turned to the recent enemies of Pictland, the Northumbrians, for help in introducing Roman Easter and the Roman tonsure into his kingdom. It is therefore equally likely that he would have enlisted the help of the less conservative wing of the Irish or Columban church for the same ends. The fact that he did not introduce Northumbrian clergy into Kinrimonth is scarcely surprising, given that the province of Fife had only recently been recovered from Northumbrian domination, after the battle of Dunnichen in 685.

Even more politically sensitive would have been Fothrif or west Fife and adjacent territories. Only a short stretch of water separated these from Northumbrian-held Lothian, and from Abercorn WLO, the centre of a short-lived bishopric set up by King Egfrith for his Pictish conquests (see Bede *Historia Ecclesiastica* IV.26).

In a recent re-assessment of the Latin *Life of St Serf*, Alan Macquarrie confirms Serf's credentials as a Pictish saint, and tentatively suggests that he filled the vacuum north of the Forth left by the flight of the Anglian bishop Trumwine from his seat at Abercorn after 685 (Macquarrie, 1993, *passim*, especially 133). The church in this area would seem to be under direct Pictish control, which explains both the absence of *cill*-names, in stark contrast to east Fife, and the presence of several places containing what I hope I have been able to show is a Pictish and (north) Cumbric word for church, *both* or *bod*.

Macquarrie goes on to suggest that in filling this vacuum along the shores of the Forth, Serf was at the same time 'reorganising the church ... along the lines of the Gaelic church' (Macquarrie, 1993, 133). It is more likely that, if Serf was indeed re-establishing the church north of the Forth after 685, he would have organised it along Roman and Pictish lines, under the close scrutiny of the Pictish kings.

Serf's *Life* opens with a long section associating him with lands around the Mediterranean. This included a spell as pope, before, through divine intervention, he decides to swap Rome for Culross. What we may be seeing here is some kind of symbolic portrayal of Serf's allegiance to a Roman party within the late seventh- or early eighth-century church.

* * * *

I would now like to widen out the focus again to include all of eastern Scotland, and to ask the question: do other *cill* and *both* names throughout former Pictland support any of the above hypothesis regarding their distribution in Fife and Fothrif?

The five *cill*-names in Atholl are all within a few miles of each other, and are all clustered around the important secular and church centre of Logierait, at the junction of the Tay and the Tummel. Beyond this tight knot are another three or four in neighbouring areas both to the east and the west. Most of these are listed in Appendix 2.2. The earliest forms of Logierait are *Login Mahedd* etc.

(e.g. *RRS* ii no.336, dated 1189x95). It almost certainly contains the name of St Coeddi, bishop of Iona, who died in 712, and was a signatory of *Cáin Adamnáin*, otherwise known as the Law of Innocents (Watson, 1926, 314). As with Dúnchad above, this is another link with Iona, and Adomnán, around 700.

Logie Mahedd was the chief church of Atholl, situated at Rait, which was the *caput* of Atholl (*Scone Liber* no.55). Logie Mahedd's association with at least some of these surrounding *cill*-names is not purely one of geographical proximity. A late twelfth-century charter, by which Earl Malcolm of Atholl grants the church of Logie Mahedd to Scone Abbey, lists three of the nearby *cill*-names as chapels belonging to Logie (RRS ii no.336).

Noteworthy also is the place-name Ardeonaig on the south shore of Loch Tay, with its associated church of Cill-mo-Charmaig. This was the name of a medieval parish, and was originally *Ardoueny* (1275, Bagimond's Roll 73), later *Ardewnan* (*RMS* ii no.2235), and contains the name Adomnán. Douglas MacLean suggests that the saint's name in Cill-mo-Charmaig may in fact be a hypocoristic form of Columba himself (MacLean, 1983, 60). I would not want to press this too far, as hypocorism can cover a multitude of sins. What is more certain is that Ardeonaig contains the name of Adomnán. Nor is it the only place-name to contain 'Adomnán' in this area. Watson (1926, 270-71) lists two in neighbouring Glen Lyon, and one by Grantully in Strath Tay; while the important early church centre of Dull, also in Strath Tay, had Adomnán as patron saint.

All this, taken along with various later traditions associating Adomnán with the area, does suggest the active presence, if not of Adomnán himself, then at the very least of his close associates or devotees at the heart of Atholl. It is, I would contend, no coincidence that it is in this very area where, in contrast to other parts of Perthshire and central eastern Scotland, we have such a proliferation of the *cill*-element.

A detailed analysis of the cluster of *cill*-names around Rosemarkie in Easter Ross and south-east Sutherland has still to be undertaken, although it is tempting to see them in conjunction with that famous, if shadowy, figure Curadán-Boniface, bishop of Rosemarkie, contemporary of Adomnán, and another signatory of Adomnán's Law of Innocents. It would seem that, like Adomnán himself, he was a Romaniser. For more on Curadán, see Watson,

1926, 315; and MacDonald, 1992, *passim*.

In summary, my hypothesis is that the establishment of these three clusters of *cill*-names in eastern Scotland was a result of Columban and/or Irish intervention in support of the Romanising tendencies within the Pictish kingdom in the late seventh and early eighth century. The presence of the place-name element *both* in an ecclesiastical context points, however, more towards direct Pictish or British spheres of influence, possibly within the same historical context as *cill*.

Nevertheless, in the case of the eastern *cill*-clusters, whatever they might have in common from an onomastic or historical point of view, there is one important factor which separates the east Fife cluster from those of Atholl and Easter Ross. That is accessibility from Dál Riata. Atholl lies at the eastern end of one of the few major crossing points of Druim Alban, by Strathfillan and Glen Dochart to Loch Tay. The name 'Atholl' alone, which means New Ireland, and is first recorded in 739 (see Watson, 1926, 228-9), suggests major early settlement from the west, long before the general establishment of Scottish power in Pictland in the ninth century. Furthermore the *Amra Choluimb Chille*, the famous elegy to Columba written within a few years of his death, twice mentions Columba as working amongst tribes of the Tay (6).

Easter Ross lies at the eastern end of the Great Glen, the chief link between Dál Riata and east northern Scotland, and the route we know Columba took on several occasions (see Anderson, 1961, §§74b-75b, 79b-82a and 114b-115a). There is in fact a trail of *cill*-names which leads from Dál Riata to Easter Ross along this important thoroughfare.

So both these areas - Atholl and Easter Ross - could well have been open to important Columban influence during the life-time of Columba himself, over a century before 700. This very early contact may have played its part in the creation of the unusually high number of *cill*-names in these two areas. So whatever else this means, it does make the cluster of *cill*-names in east Fife even more exceptional.

In any final analysis, which I am in no position to attempt here, we would have to take into consideration other features which make Fife special in the Pictish period, the most striking being the marked lack of Class I and Class II

Pictish stones relative to other parts of Pictland (7).

I referred above to the rich seam of ecclesiastical place-name elements in Scotland, and the brief glimpse which this discussion provides shows just how rich a seam it is, even in a relatively unrefined form. There is much more work to be done, however, before place-names can make their full contribution to our understanding of the spread, structure, organisation and allegiances of the early church in Scotland.

St Andrews Scottish Studies Institute
University of St Andrews

I am grateful to Dr Thomas Clancy for his comments on this text.

Appendix 1

Both/bod in ecclesiastical contexts

Scotland

1 Parishes containing *bod* or *both* in Strathclyde and Lennox.
BALDERNOCK STL (*[B]uthernok & Buthirnok c.*1200; *Bothornok* 1532)
BALFRON STL (*Buthbren* 1233)
BONHILL DNB (*Buthelulle c.*1270; *Bothlul* 1273)
BOTHWELL LAN (*Botheuill* 1242)

2 Parishes containing *both* in Pictland.
BALQUHIDDER PER (*Bu[t]hfyder c.*1268)
BETHELNIE now Meldrum par. ABD (*Buthelny c.*1220; *Bothelny* 1452)
BOHARM BNF originally a chapel of Arndilly (*Bocharnye* 1426)
BOTARIE now Cairnie par. ABN (*Butharryn* 1232)
BOTRIPHNIE BNF (*Buthrothyn & Buttruthin* 1226)
TULLIBODY CLA (*Dunbodeuin* 1147; *Tulibodeuin* 1164; *Tulibo[th]en' c.*1168)
TULLIBOLE KNR (*Tulybothwyn* 1217; *Tulibotheuile & Tulibothwin* 1227)

Note also
BOTHAN par. now Yester par. ELO (*Bothan c.*1250)

BOTHKENNAR par. now in Grangemouth par. STL (*Buthkenner c.*1250)
SHAMBOTHY † CLA (*Sc(h)embothy c.*1350, *Schandbody* 1490)

3 Chapel sites etc. containing *both* in Pictland.
BATH Culross par. FIF (formerly PER detached): (*Baith Estir & Westir* 1540; *Westir Both* 1543; *Chapeltoun of Both* 1587).
BOATH Carmylie par. ANG: the chapel of St Laurence situated on the land of *Konanmorcapil* (part of the lands of Conon) is described as the chapel "*del Both*'" 1276 x 88 (*Arb. Lib.* i no.247).
BOITH †, Panbride par. ANG: the chapel of *Boith* was granted to church of Brechin, by Bishop Adam of Brechin in 1348; it was stipulated with this grant that vicar of adjacent Monikie par. was to say a mass of St Mernóc ('missam de beato Marnoco') every Sunday (*Brech. Reg.* i no.8); with this chapel went land of *Botmernok* in the feudal holding of Panmuir, Panbride par., 'the *both* of St Mernóc' (*Brech. Reg.* i no.11).
BORENICH, Blair Atholl par. PER: occurs with variation in the generic between *both* and *mòine* (?) as *Montrainyche* alias *Disart* 1509; *Borannych* 1512. This alias implies an early religious association (Gaelic *dìseart* 'hermitage').

Note also 'capella de *Branboth*' in Glen Lyon PER *St A. Lib.* 295-6 1214x29. See also Cowan, 1967, under Killinlynar. Watson (1926, 312), however, derives this from a genitive of the personal name Branub.

Wales

4 Parishes containing *bod*
BODEDERN Angelsey (Edern son of Nudd)
BODELWYDDAN Flintshire
BODFARI Flintshire
BODWROG Angelsey (Twrog)
BOTFFORDD Angelsey

Ireland

5 Parishes containing *both*
BODONEY Co. Tyrone (*domhnach;* see above p.98)
BOHO Co. Fermanagh (plural *botha*)
BOHOLA Co. Mayo (St Tola)
RAPHOE Co. Donegal (*ràth* + *both*)

SHANBOGH Co. Kilkenny (*seann* 'old').

1 *cill*-names in Fife

FETTYKILL (now Leslie par.) (*Fithkil c.*1175) - 'wood kirk' (Gaelic *fiodh*).
KILCONQUHAR par. (*Kilcunkath c.*1200)- Dúnchad (Duncan).
KILDUNCAN, Kingsbarns par. (*Kyldonquhane* 1382) - Dúnchad (Duncan).
KILGOUR (now Falkland par.) (*Kilgouerin* 1224) - ? burn-name.
KILMANY par. (*Kilmannin* 1202) - ?
KILMARON, Cupar par. (*Kilmaron c.*1220) - Rón.
KILMINNING, Crail par. (*Kilmonane* 1452) - Móinenn.
KILRENNY par. (*Kilrethni c.*1170) - ? Ethernan (of the Isle of May).
KINGLASSIE par. (*Kilglessin c.*1155) - Gaelic *glais* 'burn, stream'.
KINGLASSIE, St Andrews & St Leonards par. (*Kynglessyn c.*1220) - ditto
METHIL (medieval) par. (*Methkil* 1207) - 'mid(dle) kirk' (Gaelic *meadhon*).

2 Some *cill*-names in Atholl PER.

FORTINGALL par. (*Forterkil* 1214x49)
KILLIECHANGIE, Logierait par. (*capella de Kelchemi c.*1190) - Cóemhi.
KILLIECHASSIE, Weem par. (*capella de Kelkassin c.*1190) - Cassian.
KILLICHONAN, medieval par. aka Rannoch, now in Fortingall PER - Conn(án).
KILMAVEONAIG, medieval par., now Blair Atholl par. (*Kilmeuenoc* 1275)- ? Beoghna, second abbot of Bangor, died 606 (Watson, 1926, 310).
KILMICHEL of Tulliemet, Logierait par. (*capella de Kelmichel de T. c.*1190)- Michael.
KILMICHEL, now Kirkmichael par. (*Kylmichel* 13th c.) - Michael.
KILMORICH, Dunkeld & Dowally par. - ? Muireadhach.

Note also: LOGIERAIT, formerly *Login Mahedd c.*1190 - Coeddi.

Abbreviations

County Abbreviations

ABD Aberdeenshire
ANG Angus
BNF Banffshire
CLA Clackmannanshire
DNB Dunbartonshire
ELO East Lothian
FIF Fife
LAN Lanarkshire
KNR Kinross-shire
PER Perthshire
STL Stirlinghshire
WLO West Lothian

Other Abbreviations

Arb. Lib.	*Liber S. Thome de Aberbrothoc*, Bannatyne Club 1848-56.
Bagimond's Roll	*SHS* Misc. vi, pp.3-77, ed. A.I. Dunlop 1939.
Brech. Reg.	*Registrum Episcopatus Brechinensis*, Bannatyne Club 1856.
CSSR iv	*Calendar of Scottish Supplications to Rome*, vol. 4 (1433-47), ed. A.I. Dunlop & D. MacLauchlan 1983.
DES	*Discovery and Excavation in Scotland.*
ECMS	*Early Christian Monuments of Scotland*, J. Romilly Allen & J. Anderson, 1903 (reprinted in 2 volumes, Pinkfoot Press, 1993).
ES	*Early Sources of Scottish History 500 to 1286*, ed. A. O. Anderson 1922.
par.	parish
RMS	*Registrum Magni Sigilli Regum Scottorum* edd. J.M. Thomson & others 1882-1914.

RRS ii — *Regesta Regum Scottorum* vol.ii, (*Acts of William I*) ed. G.W.S. Barrow 1971.

Scone Liber — *Liber Ecclesie de Scon*, Bannatyne & Maitland Clubs 1843.

St A. Lib. — *Liber Cartarum Prioratus Sancti Andree in Scotia*, Bannatyne Club 1841.

Notes

1 For the most comprehensive list of Celtic ecclesiastical place-name elements in Scotland, see Watson, 1926, 244-69.

2 See for example A. MacDonald, '"*Annat*' in Scotland: A Provisional Review', *Scottish Studies* vol. 17 (1973), 135-46; T.O. Clancy, '*Annat* in Scotland and the origins of the parish', *Innes Review*, forthcoming; A. MacDonald, 'Gaelic *cill (Kil(l)-)* in Scottish Place-Names', *Bulletin of the Ulster Place-Name Society* vol.2 (1979), 9-19; Nicolaisen, 1976, 108-111 (for *kirk*); and 128 ff (for *cill*); G.W.S. Barrow, 'The Childhood of Scottish Christianity: a Note on Some Place-Name Evidence', *Scottish Studies* vol.27 (1983), 1-15 (for *eglēs); J. MacQueen, 'The Gaelic Speakers of Galloway and Carrick', *Scottish Studies* vol. 17 (1973), 17-33 (for *cill* and *kirk* in Galloway).

3 For more details of these names, see Appendix 2.1. See also Taylor, 1995.

4 These are a) Kilmuir (*Cill Moire* 'church of Mary'), a medieval parish, now part of Brechin par. ANG (Kilmor 1274 Bagimond's Roll 52; mistranscribed as *Kyrimur* 1275 *ibid*. 69). In 1473 it is referred to as the church of the Blessed Virgin Mary of *Kilmore* next to Brechin. The church was situated between the cathedral and the castle (National Grid Reference NO597 600). Note that the only carving of the motif of the Virgin and Child in early medieval Scotland, apart from Iona, and Kildalton, Islay, comes from a Class III stone from Brechin (Smyth, 1984, 126 and *ECMS* vol.2, 249-50).
b) Burghill, a medieval parish, now part of Brechin par. ANG (church of *Buthirkill*' c.1250 *Arb. Lib.* i no.300 (p.241); *Botherkill* c.1250 *RMS* ii no.1358; *Bouregill* 1473 *RMS* ii no.1102). It is almost certainly the parish of St Tevanan of *Unthiekil* which appears as a prebend in the church of Brechin in 1446 (*CSSR* iv no.1290; see also Cowan, 1967, under Unthiekil). The first element is

probably Gaelic *bothar*, Old Irish *bóthar*, 'road, lane'.

5 For more on Fothrif, its extent and usage, see Taylor, 1995, 20-7.

6 See Clancy and Márkus, 1995, 104-5 and 112-3; for discussion see 118-9.

7 See, for example, the distribution map in Stevenson, 1955, 100. To this must be added three more Class I stones, from the parishes of Collessie, Falkland and Strathmiglo respectively. The two shown on Stevenson's map are from Lindores, Abdie par., and Walton, Cults par.. All five lie within the same swathe of country north or north-east of the Lomonds in parishes on either side of the boundary between the medieval deaneries of Fife and Fothrif. See *ECMS* vol.2, 343-4; Jackson, 1989, 32-3; and *DES*, 1989, 17.

References

Anderson, A.O. and M.O., 1961, *Adomnan's Life of Columba*.

Anderson, M.O., 1974, 'St Andrews before Alexander I', *The Scottish Tradition* ed. G.W.S. Barrow, 1-13.

Clancy, T.O. and Márkus, G., 1995, *Iona: The Earliest Poetry of a Celtic Monastery*.

Cowan, I.B., 1967, *The Parishes of Medieval Scotland*, Scottish Record Society, vol.93.

Flanagan, D., 1982, 'A Summary Guide to the more commonly attested ecclesiastical elements in place-names [with special reference to Northern Ireland]', *Bulletin of the Ulster Place-Name Society*, series 2 vol.4, 69-75.

Jackson, A., 1989, *The Pictish Trail*.

Joyce, P.W., 1869, *The Origin and History of Irish Names of Places*, vol. 1.

MacDonald, A., 1992, *Curadán, Boniface and the early church of Rosemarkie*.

MacDowall, C.G., 1963, *The Chanonry of Ross*.

MacLean, D., 1983, *Scottish Studies* vol.27, 53-65

Macquarrie, A., 1993, '*Vita Sancti Servani:* The Life of St Serf', *Innes Review* vol.44 (2) 122-52.

Nicolaisen, W.F.H., 1976, *Scottish Place-Names* (second impression with additional information 1979).

Padel, O.J., 1985, *Cornish Place-Name Elements*.

Smyth, A.P., 1984, *Warlords and Holy Men*.

Stevenson, R.B.K., 1955, 'Pictish Art', *The Problem of the Picts* ed. F.T. Wainwright, 97-128.

Taylor, R.S., 1995, 'Settlement-names in Fife', unpublished PhD, University of Edinburgh.

Watson, W.J., 1926, *The History of the Celtic Place-Names of Scotland*.

Iona, Scotland, and the Céli Dé

Thomas Owen Clancy

Although recent scholarship has illuminated a great deal about the crucial period in Scottish history from around 800 to 950, there remains much work to be done (Anderson 1980; Smyth 1984; Broun 1994). This paper aims to investigate two aspects of the evolution of the church in Scotland during this period. First of all, I wish to address the question of the history of Iona and its abbots in the years following the building of Kells. Second, I will be investigating the widespread presence in Scotland in the later middle ages of the groups of clerics known as *céli Dé*, 'clients of God', by first asking questions about their origins. I will begin by looking at the career of one person, a neglected abbot of Iona about whom some fairly certain things can be said, and then proceed to some much more speculative arguments. My approach to some of the Scottish sources, as will become apparent, is optimistic: I take some material such as king-lists and chronicles as being more or less reliable. In some senses, then, my analysis later in the paper will be based on a best-case scenario for the interpretation of the sources.

A mythology has grown up in scholarly accounts about the effects of the early Viking raids on Iona, which assumes that, having built the new Irish monastery of Kells between 807 and 814, Iona was effectually abandoned, leaving a hole in relationships between the Columban *familia* and royal power in Scotland only rectified in 849 with the transfer of some of Columba's relics to the new church of Dunkeld built by Cináed mac Alpín (for instance, Smyth 1984, 147, 185-8). This cannot be supported by the evidence we have from Irish annals. The view that leaders of the Columban community abandoned Iona for Kells in 814 has been recently rejected by both Máire Herbert and John Bannerman (Herbert 1988, 70-3; Bannerman 1993, 29-33), but there is room for further exploration of the role of Iona in Irish and Scottish politics in the first half of the ninth century.

Alongside the gap in our understanding of religious history at this period left by the story of the semi-abandonment of Iona, we may place the mysterious success in Scotland of the religious reform movement associated with the name of the *céli Dé*. This movement is primarily associated with the south of Ireland, but by 943 we find Constantín son of Áed, king of Scots, retiring to become abbot of the *céli Dé* community in Cennrígmonaid (Kinrimond, later St Andrews), and by the twelfth century we become aware—through charters and other church records—of the astonishing prevalence of *céli Dé* communities throughout Scotland (ES i, 446-8; Anderson 1974, 2-3; Anderson 1980, 283; Reeves 1864). We know next to nothing about how this reform movement was introduced into Scotland, let alone why its success was so pervasive here. Indeed, there has been little new research into the *céli Dé* in Scotland since Reeves produced his study in 1864 (but see Anderson 1974, 2-3; Miller 1982, 140-3; MacQuarrie 1992).

This paper aims to address both these problems in Scottish history, and to suggest that the influence of the *céli Dé* in Scotland is at least partly connected with the actions of a much-neglected figure, Diarmait *alumnus* (fosterson or pupil) of Daigre, abbot of Iona from 814 to sometime after 831.

Diarmait is an important figure and one about whom a fair amount can be known, and hence his neglect by scholars is the more inexplicable. Only two causes for this occur to me. One is that he falls between two perceived watersheds in the history of the Columban *familia*. The building of Kells is one of these watersheds, and Diarmait is the first abbot of Iona after its completion, and hence does not figure in the study of Iona abbots in the Andersons' editions of the Life of Columba (Anderson and Anderson 1991, xliii-xliv). So too, he comes before the other watershed, the presumed splitting of Columba's relics between Dunkeld and Kells, and thus, for instance, comes outside the parameters of Bannerman's recent study (Bannerman 1993). Falling between these stools as he does, his significance has gone unappreciated. The other possible explanation is his lack of both obit and genealogy: he is the only abbot of Iona whose date of death is unknown to us. It may be that he died outside Ireland, or indeed outside the British Isles. Perhaps, like his successor, he went on pilgrimage to Rome, though one presumes that he was not murdered *en route* by Englishmen as his successor was (See AU 854). Either way, he ceases to be visible after 831. Added to this, we do not even know his father's name, only the name of his fosterfather or teacher, Daigre, about whom in turn we know nothing.

Of his career, however, the annals give us some information (See Appendix, 1). So we know he took over the abbacy of Iona when Cellach retired in 814. The entry in the Annals of Ulster which refers to this event has sometimes been read as if it was the abbacy of Kells Diarmait took over, but this is not what it says (e.g. Smyth 1984, 147; this is under influence of the entry for 807 in the later 'Dublin Annals of Innisfallen', cf. ES i, 259). Indeed, there is little clear evidence that Cellach himself, the founder of Kells, was ever its abbot, let alone Diarmait, though it has been seen as likely that the abbacy of Kells stayed in the hands of abbots of Iona for the first phase of its existence (Herbert 1988, 70-4; Bannerman 1993, 32). As far as Diarmait is concerned, every record we possess referring to him, and there are many, call him abbot of Iona.

Diarmait was abbot during a turbulent period in the history of the Columban *familia*. Violence was to be found from domestic sources as well as from Viking raids. The king of the Uí Néill, Áed mac Néill (Áed Oirdnide) of the Cenél nEógain, seems to have been involved in the killing of the head of Adomnán's foundation of Raphoe in 817. This must have been felt as a severe betrayal by the Columban familia, since Áed's father Niall Frossach had died in pilgrimage on Iona in 778. That same year, 817, the community of Columba went to Tara to excommunicate Áed. He died two years later, and we do not know if he was ever reconciled with Columba's monks. Indeed, the Annals of Innisfallen tell us, intriguingly, that he died on a hosting in Scotland, which is where the abbot of Iona had gone in 818 (AI, CS, but see AU 819, and Kelleher 1971, 122-3). This incident may have helped hasten the Columban community's shift of interest towards the southern Uí Néill dynasty of Clann Cholmáin, and away from their earlier northern patrons.

We know of two sojourns of Diarmait in Scotland. We must remember that this is a somewhat Hiberno-centric perspective, and had we Scottish chronicles his times spent in Ireland might well be regarded as 'journeys'. The first was in 818, and we do not know its duration. The second was from 829 to 831. In 818, *Chronicon Scotorum* notes that he went "with the *sgrín* of Colum Cille". In 829 we are told that he went with the insignia/relics (*mínd*) of Columba, returning with them in 831. What these relics were is uncertain, though they may have been the bones of Columba. Columba's shrine was described as existing on Iona in 825 in Walahfrid Strabo's poem about Blathmac mac Flainn's fatal defence of it (ES i, 263-5). However, it is possible that the relics had travelled to Kells for the consecration of its church in 814, and that they were being returned to Iona in 818. (This was possibly for safekeeping, since in 818 Áed mac Néill may have seemed a more ominous threat than the Norse. The Annals of Innisfallen record in the same year the journey of the abbot of

Louth to Munster with St Mochta's shrine in flight from Áed. See Kelleher 1971, 122-3.) Columba's relics may have stayed in Iona, perhaps being removed to Kells after Blathmac's martyrdom, and travelling with Diarmait on his 829-831 journey. (On terminology of shrines and *scrín Choluim Chille*, see Bannerman 1993, 18ff.)

On the other hand, Diarmait's two trips coincide with the reigns of two important kings of both Dál Riata and the Picts, Constantín son of Fergus (790?-820) and his brother and successor Óengus (820-834). To each of these kings the foundation or building of a church is assigned in the king-lists: to Constantín, Dunkeld; to Óengus, Kinrimond (St Andrews) (Anderson 1980, 266; see Appendix 2ab). This latter, if the source is believable, must denote the building of a church or the setting up of a new community, since we know of the existence of a monastery at Kinrimond in 747 (AU). While it would be incautious to jump to conclusions about Diarmait's involvement in these alleged foundations, there is every likelihood that he was.

The movement of the relics of Columba would not have been undertaken lightly, and some important purpose, such as the consecration of a church, must have led to Diarmait's journeys. Indeed, considering that Diarmait's successor Indrechtach was probably involved in the next phase of Dunkeld's consecration, in 849, it is almost impossible not to connect the transport of Columba's shrine in 818, with the attribution to Constantín of Dunkeld. One may note that the annal entries for 831 and 849 are very similar, and it is only as a result of the information in the Scottish Chronicle that we conclude that anything extraordinary happened in 849 (see Appendix 1, 2d). It is only by inferrence (no doubt a correct one) that we connect the two events, and judge that the relics which Indrechtach brought back to Ireland were partial, some of them going to Cináed's new church in Dunkeld. A similar inferrence is, I would argue, sensible in interpreting the conjunction of the transportation of the relics of Columba to Scotland by Diarmait in 818 and the founding or building of Dunkeld by Constantín.

Likewise the foundation or building of a church in Kinrimond during Óengus' reign could well be one reason for Diarmait's Scottish journey of 829-831, though we may note that St Andrews has no explicit Columban connections and a monastery was there already in the eighth century. Simon Taylor has already detailed the dedications to Iona abbots and bishops which occur in the vicinity of St Andrews, though these probably belong to an earlier period (see Taylor, above). As we shall see, St Andrews' connections with the *céli Dé* make the association with Diarmait all the more likely.

Already, then, the annals argue for a prominent role for Diarmait in the events of his time, both in Ireland and Scotland. However, it is from an entirely different, and untapped source, that we learn about another aspect of Diarmait's career: his involvement with and influence on the monastic reforms of the *céli Dé*. The document usually called 'The Monastery of Tallaght' was written sometime in the middle of the ninth century (MT, 120-2). It is a compilation of the customs and sayings primarily of Máel Ruain, founder of Tallaght, and his disciples, but it includes traditions from other monastics who were either influential in or influenced by the reform. The author drew heavily on testimony from one of the pupils of Máel Ruain, Máel Dithruib, once a monk at Tallaght, and latterly at Terryglass, where he died in 841 (AFM, 840). It has been commented that:

> the notes have the appearance of being due to a monastic Boswell whose Johnson was Máel-Dithruib. The phraseology suggests that the compiler was not writing at Tamlachta, but perhaps at Tír-dá-glas. (Kenney, 472)

The author of 'The Monastery of Tallaght' had a particular interest in the customs of Iona monks, although his knowledge of them was perhaps second-hand (MT, §§47, 52, 65, 66, 68, 69, 80, 85; excerpts in Appendix 4). Prominent in the text is the name of Diarmait, abbot of Iona, and some of the passages make it clear that he was in direct contact with Terryglass monks, and hence was probably himself the ultimate source of the Iona information contained in the document. For instance we are told that Diarmait left three words with Carthach, bishop and abbot of Terryglass (†853) (MT §47). Another passage which paraphrases the words of Máel Dithruib incorporates an anecdote about the customs of an unnamed abbot of Iona, and it seems likely that this anecdote came through Máel Dithruib and ultimately from Diarmait (MT §52, and see §85). There is some suggestion that the document was composed after Diarmait's death (MT, 122). The editors of the text also suggest that it was substantially composed before the death of Máel Dithruib in 840. If both these hypotheses are correct, we could surmise that Diarmait died between 831 and 840.

From this document we learn of the existence in ninth-century Iona of something called the 'Rule of Columba', and we know of some of its contents. So for instance we are told:

> In Colum Cille's Rule Saturday's ration is the same as Sunday's, on account of the honour paid to the Sabbath in the Old Testament. It is only in respect of work that it is distinguished from Sunday. (MT §69)

We should perhaps not think of the Rule as being a written document *per se*, but rather the customs and usages of Iona, which may or may not have been committed to writing. This Rule, whatever its form, was adaptable by the abbot of the day. In one passage we learn the way in which Diarmait would vary the Rule:

> Colum Cille, however, kept three fasts in the year, with a half ration on each of them, and this half ration was liberal. As an equivalent of fasting, Diarmait used to allow two exactly equal rations to be made, whether it happened to be coarse or light food, and one of these to be given to God; the other he was to eat himself; and this serves in place of a fast. (MT §80)

We even learn interesting details, such as that Iona kept, sometime after Easter, a festival called the Feast of the Ploughmen, something perhaps equivalent to the Jewish feast of first fruits (MT §68, and see note, 172). From an anecdote, too, we hear of Adomnán's intervention in a dispute over the abbacy of Clonmacnois, a remarkable event if true (MT §85; Etchingham 1993, 155).

We learn that Diarmait also had connections with Clonmacnois. An anecdote, likely to have been told to the Terryglass source first-hand, tells how Diarmait and Blathmac mac Flainn (the Blathmac who was martyred in 825) were cautioned by one Colcu that they needed to be reconsecrated by a bishop after having had a man called Cú Ruí die in their arms (MT §65). Colcu may be the Clonmacnois scholar Colcu úa Duinechda (†796 AU) and it is probable that Cú Ruí is the king of Cenél Loegaire, a minor midland sept of the Uí Néill (†797 AU, 792 AFM). If this anecdote has any historicity, and if my identification of the figures in this vignette is correct, then both Diarmait and Blathmac mac

Flainn were active in the Irish midlands in the late eighth century.

Some sort of Rule of Columba, therefore, existed in the early ninth century, and mediated through Diarmait, the well-respected abbot of Iona, it was influential on some of the *céli Dé* reformers. Diarmait is seen in turn taking advice from one of them, Colcu. Blathmac, later to be martyred, was also remembered respectfully by the reformers. Iona, it is clear, was thoroughly involved in this movement of monastic reform. If this paper demonstrates nothing else, the existence of this potent and obvious link between Iona and the reformers, and between the Iona abbot and Scotland, should be clear.

In many ways this connection between Iona and southern Ireland mirrors the earlier efforts at codifying church structure and practice which united the skills of two monks from Iona and the Lismore daughter-house of Dairinis in the compilation of the *Collectio Canonum Hibernensis* (Wasserschleben 1885; Clancy and Márkus 1995, 30-1). The *céli Dé* reform seems initially to radiate out from a triangle composed of Lismore, Dairinis and Daire Eidnech (O'Dwyer 1981, 46). It is particularly notable that Máel Ruain's teacher and mentor, Fer-Dá-Crích, was abbot of Dairinis (†747, AU; O'Dwyer 1981, 30). He may well have been a monk there while the *Hibernensis* was being compiled in a joint project between Iona and Dairinis scholars. The *Hibernensis* itself was clearly influential on some of the literature of the *céli Dé* (O'Dwyer 1981, 4).

Diarmait's involvement with the *céli Dé* gives us an extremely plausible basis for understanding the spread of the movement which must have occurred in Scotland. It is notable that the three most prominent Columban houses in Scotland and Ireland in the ninth century—Iona, Kells and, traditionally, Dunkeld—had, by the eleventh and twelfth centuries, communities of *céli Dé* incorporated in them (on Dunkeld, see MacQuarrie 1992, 122-3). Though we know nothing about when these communities were established, it may be significant that Columban monasteries which later rose to prominence, such as Derry, do not seem to have had *céli Dé*. It may well be, then, that these communities were established hard on the heels of the reform movement. Kinrimond may have had a community by the mid-tenth century. It is worth considering that if the ninth-century dates are correct for Dunkeld and Kinrimond, then they take their place among a number of newly founded or newly prominent monasteries associated with the *céli Dé*, such as Tallaght and Roscrea. We could conjecture that whatever the nature of the ninth-century foundations of Dunkeld and Kinrimond, communities of *céli Dé* may have been established there. What would these communities have been like?

This is not the place to go into great detail about *céli Dé* customs and practices (see O'Dwyer 1981; Reeves 1864; Hughes 1966, 173-93). In short, it is accurate enough to call this a monastic reform, dedicated to the renewal of the coenobitic lifestyle. Although there is, as has been noticed by scholars, a marked increase in the number of anchorites at this stage in the annals, it is somewhat less than accurate to describe the *céli Dé* as an anchoritic, or even simply an ascetic movement. All the documentation makes it clear that the *céli Dé* lived in communities and served under rules. Later notices of their communities, existing within larger monasteries oriented primarily towards pastoral care or property management or political games, make it clear that within this mixed development called the monastery, they were the true monks (See Herbert 1994, 68-9).

But the documentation of the reform makes it clear that they were not simply concerned with interior reform of monastic communities or ascetic discipline within them. They were also deeply interested in promoting those proper orientations and structures for church government and pastoral care which had been a main concern of ecclesiastical legislators in the eighth century. (On such 'prescriptive texts', see Charles-Edwards 1992.) The *Prose Rule of the Céli Dé* incorporates the idea of the contract for provision of pastoral care found in the eighth-century *Ríagail Phátraic* (Reeves, 211-15; O'Keeffe). Other rules from this period seem to draw on the *Hibernensis* (O'Dwyer 1981, 4). The *Rule of Mo Chutu*, the *céli Dé* stance of which is clearly seen in the use of the first person plural when discussing the responsibilities of the *céli Dé*, begins by setting out the responsibilities of bishops and also discusses priests and confessors (Meyer 1906). It is worth noting that the ninth-century records of reforming monasteries include many bishops among their personnel, often serving conjointly as abbot, and Máel Ruain himself was a bishop (Tallaght: 792, 812, 874; Finglas: 812, 838, 867; Castledermot: 843, all AU). Though the *céle Dé* himself would not necessarily be involved in pastoral care, nevertheless, the right-ordering of the church depended on each member performing his task, and the very possibility of ascetic detachment demanded a peaceful and well-functioning church.

One of the key themes of the prescriptive documents of the eighth century is the question of what 'ennobles' or 'frees' a given church (the Gaelic term is *sóerad*). The Munster church-tract *Bretha Nemed Toísech* sets out the church's rights and responsibilities thus:

> What are the good qualifications ennobling (*sóertho*: 'which free') a church? It is not difficult: the shrine of a righteous man, the relics of saints, divine scripture, a sinless superior, devout monks; the seven gifts of the Holy Ghost, the seven grades of the church with their divisions and with their proper functions being in it; people praying for those who serve it...penitents attending the sacrifice under the direction of a confessor with pious sayings...
>
> What are the disqualifications debasing a church (*dóertho*: 'which make it base')? It is not difficult: being without baptism, without communion, without mass, without praying for the dead, without preaching, without penitents... water through it onto the altar...misappropriation, private property, complaining, providing for clients...reddening it with blood, putting it under a lord...giving it as payment to a lord or a kin. (Breatnach 1989, 8-11)

One of the key reform texts, the ninth-century *Prose Rule of the Céli Dé*, incorporates considerations of a like nature:

> The ennobling (*sóerad*) of a church of God (lies in) baptism and communion and the singing of the intercession, with students for reading, with the offering of the body of Christ upon every altar. It is not entitled to tithes, nor to a heriot cow, nor to the third of an *andóit*, nor to the payment of a *sét* from treasures, unless its reciprocal duties of the church are in it, with regard to baptism, and communion and singing of intercession for her *manaig* (church clients/'parishioners': see Sharpe, 1992, 102) both living and dead, and there is mass upon every altar on Sundays and solemnities, and there is proper furniture on each altar. No church which does not have its proper equipment is entitled to the full tribute of the church of God, but 'a den of thieves and robbers' is its name according to Christ. (Reeves 1864, 211-2, translation mine.)

One of the interests of eighth-century legal reformers in Munster, in Armagh and in the Iona-Dairinis project of the *Collectio Canonum Hibernensis*, then,

was the question of the relationship of church and state, of what a church must do to deserve its 'free' or 'noble' status. Without fulfilling those obligations, the church would lapse into subservient status, being ruled over by other ecclesiastic or even secular lords. These concerns were put into action by the *céli Dé* in 811, when the community of Tallaght blockaded the fair of Tailtiu as a result of Áed's violation of their sanctuary (AU, 811). The Columban community under Diarmait, as we have seen, acted on the same premise against Áed in 817. Some years earlier, another reforming cleric, Fothad na Canóine of Fahan, extracted for the clergy exemption from military hostings (AU, 804; Hughes 1966, 191-2). The already mentioned *Rule of Mo Chutu*, which is also called the *Rule of Fothad na Canóine*, includes a section on the proper conduct of Christian kings (Meyer 1906, 314-5).

In such a context it may prove worthwhile to look again at some of the activities of Scottish kings in the late ninth century with regard to the legal standing of the church. I would argue that, to the extent that these notices are reliable, they reflect the influence of eighth-century Irish church legal reform, promoted through the monastic reform of the *céli Dé*, quite likely as propagated by Iona abbots. Beyond this, some of the kings of ninth-century and tenth-century Scotland can be seen to have their own connections with the reform.

We have already seen that it is probable that Diarmait's visit to Scotland in 818 with Colum Cille's relics was connected with the foundation of Dunkeld by Constantín son of Fergus. In this regard, there is another piece of evidence connecting Constantín to the *céli Dé* reformers. In the *Martyrology of Tallaght*, composed between 828 and 833 (Ó Riain 1990, 38), under the entry for March 11, the compiler(s) felt some doubt about the identity of the St Constantín there commemorated, to the extent of questioning whether this might be the Pictish Constantín, son of Fergus (Best and Lawlor 1931, 22; see Appendix 3). So near to the date of his death, this can only be explained in terms of his reputation for holiness having spread to the community of Tallaght, and it seems sensible to presume that this reputation was based primarily on his foundation and endowment of Dunkeld. We may wonder, then, whether his commemoration in a Tallaght document suggests that Dunkeld, when initially founded, was a *céli Dé* monastery (see also MacQuarrie 1992, 122-3).

There is other evidence of Constantín's religious associations. The recently discovered inscription on the face of the Dupplin cross bears his name (Custantin filius Fircus: see Forsyth, 1995), and coupled with the iconography of the cross is a vibrant monument to Christian kingship. He is one of three Pictish kings whose name is entered in the *Liber Vitae* of Durham (Airlie 1994, 42-3), and in the so-called 'Dunkeld Litany', it is almost certainly Constantín who is invoked among the *nomina sanctorum confessorum at monachorum*, where, strikingly, his name is placed next to that of Diarmait (again, almost certainly the Iona abbot of that name) (Forbes 1872, lx).

An entry in the Scottish King-List, here quoted from King-List D, notes that Giric son of Dúngal (878-889) 'was the first to give liberty to the Scottish church, which was in servitude up to that time, after the custom and practice of the Picts' (Anderson 1980, 267; Appendix 2c). Many authors, such as Isabel Henderson and Marjorie Anderson, have noted that Pictish royal power does indeed seem to have extended into the religious arena (Henderson 1967, 82-90; Anderson 1980, 198; 1982, 120-1,127-8; Hudson 1994). Noteworthy evidence of this is the decision by Nechtan mac Derile to conform to Roman usage in Pictland, followed by his expulsion of Columban clergy. Added to this must be the overt royal foundation of churches, a habit virtually unknown in Ireland, but one which in Scotland includes Abernethy and Dunkeld, and perhaps Kinrimond. Scone and Meigle appear as 'royal' institutions, and the monastery of Brechin is 'given to God' by the Scottish king. The royal foundation of churches, the power of kings to endow and construct religious centres, continued, then, beyond Pictish times, and the action may have contained implicit proprietary rights which the new Gaelic ascendancy saw as needing reformed.

If the entry on Giric is reliable, then, I would argue that it testifies to the need to reach an accommodation between church and state under law, and that the language is in accordance with the notion of *sóerad*, 'freeing, ennobling', found in Irish legal texts of the eighth century and the reform texts of the ninth. The more specific process of exempting particular churches from particular types of tribute or duty seen first in Ireland in 951 and in the Middle Gaelic *Life of Adomnán*, and later in the *Book of Deer*, does not seem applicable to this entry (Herbert 1988, 161-2; Jackson 1972, 91-3). Rather it seems to refer to general principles such as those we find the *céli Dé* defending in Ireland in the early ninth century. Giric may then have been setting into motion a process of reform of the structures of the church.

In this context we may note that the 'Dunkeld Litany' would appear to have its origins during Giric's reign. The document has been subject to later antiquarian interference, but on cursory analysis it does appear to have a genuine ninth-century core. Amid other invocations are two which are of interest, if they are authentic:

> *Ut Episcopos, Abbates Kiledeos, et omnem populum totius Albaniae conserves et protegas.*
> *Ut Regem nostrum Girich cum exercitu suo ab omnibus inimicorum insidiis tuearis et defendas.*
> That You would preserve and protect the bishops, abbots and *céli Dé*, and all the people of the whole of *Alba* (Britain? Scotland?)
> That You would guard and defend our king Girich with his army from all the snares of his enemies. (Forbes 1872, lxiii)

Equally remarkable in this context is the agreement reached between Constantín son of Áed and the bishop, Cellach. In 906, the Scottish Chronicle in the Poppleton Manuscript tells us:

> Constantín the king and Cellach the bishop, on the Hill of Faith near the royal monastery of Scone, swore to keep the laws and disciplines of the faith and the rights of the churches and the gospels, in the same manner as the Irish (*pariter cum Scottis*). From that day that hill has merited its name: the Hill of Faith. (Anderson, 1980, 251; see Appendix 2e)

This establishment of parity between the practices of the Irish church and the Scottish church (for I believe that is how this passage should be understood) can be read with more conviction in light of what we now know about the theoretical, prescriptive basis of the legal standing of churches in the eighth and ninth centuries in Ireland. Documents from this period over and over again state their interest in proper order, in churches fulfilling their contract to their people, in the provision of pastoral care (Charles-Edwards 1992, 70-1; Etchingham 1991, 104-5). These interests were as much a part of the *céli Dé* reformers' agenda as was monastic life. Indeed, the structural changes in the Scottish church which become evident from the middle of the ninth century on may well reflect the views of the reformers. Suddenly, we find ourselves in a Scotland with visible bishops, and with Fortriu, for a time at least, having a *primepscop*, a 'chief bishop', based probably at Dunkeld (AU, 865). Other bishops, such as Cellach follow in the records through the tenth and eleventh

centuries (see Anderson 1974, 2-5).

As already noted, the reformers' concern with structure and pastoral care led at least one rule to begin with a passage describing the proper behaviour of bishops. *Ríagail Phátraic*, extensively quoted by the *Prose Rule of the Céli Dé*, states clearly that every chief territory/kingdom (*prím-túath*) should have a chief bishop (*prím-epscop*):

> There should be a chief bishop (*prím espoc*) in each chief territory in Ireland, for ordaining priests, for consecrating churches, for being confessor to rulers and church-leaders and priests, for sanctifying and blessing their children after baptism, for ordering works in every church, and training boys and girls for learning and devotion... (Reeves 1864, 213; and see Etchingham 1994)

As well as being monastic, the reformers were episcopal. What we see in late ninth- and early tenth-century Scotland may well be the fruit of *céli Dé* reform as introduced through the influential channels of the abbots of Iona and their colleagues (on this, see also Miller, 1982, 140-3).

We began with a personality, that of Diarmait, abbot of Iona from 814 to before 840. Another large figure closes this study. We have seen how Constantín son of Áed was instrumental in instituting some sort of reform of the legal standing of the church in Scotland. Helping to confirm the view that the sort of reform instituted at this period stems from the vision of the *céli Dé* is the fact that it is with his name that the first explicit mention of *céli Dé* in Scotland is connected. In 943 he retired into the monastery of Kinrimond/St Andrews, to live out his life in penitence under a monastic rule. One of the king-lists further adds the detail that he served as head of the *céli Dé* (ES i, 447-8). The royal respect and patronage this implies suggests that they in turn had been influential in the Scottish church during his lifetime. (On other *céli Dé* attributes in St Andrews, see Anderson, 1974, 1-3; Miller, 1982, 141.)

So whether all the connections I have attempted to make here are valid or not, we are left with two ends of an important period, a period which begins with an abbot of Iona, influential in the *céli Dé* reform and a sojourner in Scotland, whose travels with the relics of Columba perhaps coincided with important new foundations there. It ends with a king, influential in church reform in Scotland, who himself retires to one of the monasteries built or endowed a century before, living out his life as head of one of the reformed coenobitic communities whose ethos the abbot of Iona had helped to mould. Between those two brackets there are, I believe, good grounds for interpreting Iona, and its dealings with the Scottish royalty, as the main vehicle for the establishment of *céli Dé* reforms, monastic and structural, in the Scottish church.

Department of Celtic,
University of Edinburgh

I would like to thank John Bannerman, Gilbert Márkus and Simon Taylor for reading drafts of this paper and for helpful discussion and criticism. I am indebted to Katherine Forsyth and Colmán Etchingham for sending me copies of their work in advance of publication. This work was made possible by the British Academy, which supports the writer with a Post-Doctoral Research Fellowship.

Appendix

Documents relating to Diarmait, abbot of Iona fl. 814 x 831.

1. ANNALS

814 (AU) Cellach, abbot of Iona, having finished the construction of the church of Kells, resigned the headship, and Diarmait, fosterson (or pupil) of Daigre, was appointed in his place.

815 (AU) Cellach, son of Congal, abbot of Iona, fell asleep.

817 (AU) Máel Dúin son of Cenn Fáelad, superior of Raphoe, of the community of Columba, was slain.

Columba's community went to Tara to curse ('excommunicate') Áed.

818 (CS) Diarmait, abbot of Iona, went to Scotland with the reliquary of Colum Cille.

819 (AI) Death of Áed son of Niall, king of Tara, on a hosting in Alba. [But other annals note his death as occuring at Áth dá Ferta in Mag Conaille.]

820 (AU) Constantín son of Fergus, king of Fortriu, dies.

825 (AU) The violent death of Bla[th]mac son of Flann at the hands of the pagans in Iona.

829 (AU) Diarmait, abbot of Iona, went to Scotland with the insignia (or relics) of Columba.

831 (AU) Diarmait came to Ireland with the insignia (or relics) of Colum Cille.

849 (AU) Indrechtach, abbot of Iona, came to Ireland with the insignia (or relics) of Columba.

2. Scottish Notices on Kings and Churches:
(from Anderson 1980)
Regnal List D:

a.*Constantinus f. Fergusane xlv annis reg. Iste edificavit Dunkeldin.*
b. *Hungus f. Fergusane ix annis reg. Iste edificavit Kilremonth.*
c. *Girg mac Dungal xii a. reg. et mortuus est in Dunduin et sepultus est in Iona insula. Hic subjugavit sibi totam Yberniam [I=Berniciam] et fere totam Angliam et hic primus dedit libertatem ecclesie Scoticane qui sub servitute erat usque ad illud tempus ex consuetudine et more Pictorum.*

Giric, Dungal's son, reigned for twelve years; and he died in Dundurn, and was buried in the island of Iona. He subdued to himself all Ireland [I=Bernicia], and nearly all England; and he was the first to give liberty to the Scottish church, which was in servitude up to that time, after the custom and practice of the Picts.

Scottish Chronicle from the Poppleton MS

d. *Septimo anno regni sui reliquias sancti Columbe transportauit ad ecclesiam, quam construxit.*
In the seventh year of his (Cináed's) reign, he transported the relics of St Columba to a church which he built.
e. *Ac in .vi. anno Constantinus rex et Cellachus episcopus leges et disciplinasque fidei atque iura ecclesiarum ewangeliorumque pariter cum Scottis in colle credulitatis prope regali ciuitati Scoan deuouerunt custodire; ab hoc die collis hoc meruit nomen id est collis credulitatis.*

And in his sixth year, Constantín the king and Cellach the bishop, on the Hill of Faith (?) near the royal monastery of Scone, swore to keep the laws and disciplines of the faith and the rights of the churches and the gospels, in the same manner as the Scots. From that day that hill has merited its name: the Hill of Faith.

3. Martyrologies;

The Martyrology of Tallaght, 828x833 (Best and Lawlor 1931; Ó Riain 1990): 11 March: *Constantini Briton ‡ meic Fergusa do Cruthnechaib.*

[The feast] of Constantín the Briton (or 'of the Britons'?), or the son of Fergus, of the Picts.

4. Entries related to Diarmait in *Monastery of Tallaght*

§§ as in MT §§47, 52, 65, 66, 68, 69, 80, 85.

§47. Three words Diarmaid, abbot of Iona, left with bishop Carthach [of Terryglass, †851 AFM]: pittance, perseverance, vigil. That is, do not make a resolution, 'This is the pittance I will always eat. I will say the Beati perseveringly without desisting. This is the vigil I will always perform.'

§52.In the case of penance laid on sickly persons, this is what he (i.e. Mael-Dithruib of Terryglass) thinks right, as to the continual preparing for meals: alternate reviving and mortifying is practised on them, lest the perpetual confinement should cause their death; and if this is done, if it can be managed, without their knowledge, by telling his servant privately, 'Let a *seland* be brought to them in their pottage or on bread' (but it is more usual to bring it to them in the pottage). Once it happened that the abbot who was in Iona saw that the recluses had a bad colour. Thereupon he went to the cook and himself made the pottage for that day. He added one-third of water to the daily allowance and boiled the water. When this third had boiled away, he put a lump of butter on each man's allowance, and boiled it on the water, and then put meal over it, and so he did every day. then they noticed the change in their colour, and knew not what had caused it, since they saw the usual ration unchanged. So when their colour came back and they revived, he continued alternately to mortify and revive them from their dying state after this fashion.

§65. Now, to eat a meal with a dead man, though saintly, in the house is forbidden; but instead there are to be prayers and psalm singing on such occasions. Even one in orders who brings the sacrament to a sick man is obliged to go out of the house at once thereafter, that the sick man die not in his presence; for if he be present in the house at the death, it would not be allowable for him to peform the sacrifice until a bishop should consecrate him. It happened once on a time to Diarmait and to Blathmac mac Flaind that it was in their hands that Cú Rui expired. When he died, they were about to perform the sacrifice thereafter, without being reconsecrated, till Colcu hindered them from doing so. The authority is Leviticus [Lev 21.1-2; 11-12.]; and Diarmait also, the Abbot of Iona, agreed with him on that occasion.

§68. He does not commend fasting: he prefers a measured pittance. There is no Rule where it is imposed, except on account of injury done. There is one fast in Comgall's Rule – namely, the Wednesday before Easter. However, Colum Cille recognized three fasts only in the year: the eve of Epiphany – that is, twelve days after Christmas, and the eighth part of Colum Cille's loaf at that time, with a *seland* and a *bochtan* of good milk: that was the manner of that fast; and the first Wednesday of Lent, and the first Wednesday after Pentecost: the eighth of a loaf to each fast. However, Colum Cille relaxed the fast of the Passion for the saints of Ireland, because old men died of that fast after the long privations of Lent. A great festivity and merrymaking was regularly allowed by Colum Cille thereafter to the brethren: the growth of the crops was given to them then: three months were spent in tending and watering them. He called that the Feast of the Ploughmen, because it was then that the crops reached their full growth.

§69. In Colum Cille's Rule Saturday's ration is the same as Sunday's, on account of the honour paid to the Sabbath in the Old Testament. It is only in respect of work that it is distinguished from Sunday...

§80. Now, continual fasting was not practised by Comgall, and it is not practised by the saints at present, save one fast, namely the eve of Maundy Thursday after the Wednesday. On the eve of the Passion, however, no fast is to be observed. Colum Cille, however, kept three fasts in the year, with a half ration on each of them, and this half ration was liberal. As an equivalent of fasting, Diarmait used to allow two exactly equal rations to be made, whether it happened to be coarse or light food, and one of these to be given to God; the other he was to eat himself; and this serves in place of a fast.

Abbreviations ~~~~~~~~~~~~~~~~~~~~~~~~~~~~~~~~~~~~~~~

AFM=*The Annals of the Four Masters*, ed. John O'Donovan, Dublin, 1848-51.

AI=*The Annals of Inisfallen*, ed. Seán Mac Airt, Dublin, 1951.

AU=*The Annals of Ulster (to A.D. 1131)*, ed. Seán Mac Airt and Gearóid Mac Niocaill, Dublin, 1983.

CS=*Chronicon Scotorum*, ed. W.M. Hennessy, London, 1866.

ES=A.O. Anderson, *Early Sources of Scottish History* , 2 volumes, Edinburgh, 1922.

MT= 'The Monastery of Tallaght', ed. E.J. Gwynn and W.J. Purton, *Procedings of the Royal Irish Academy* 29C (1911) 115-179.

References ~~~~~~~~~~~~~~~~~~~~~~~~~~~~~~~~~~~~~~~

Airlie, Stuart 1994, 'The View from Maastricht', in Crawford, 33-46.

Anderson, A.O. and Anderson, M.O. 1991, *Adomnán's Life of Columba*, Oxford (revised edition).

Anderson, M.O. 1974, 'St Andrews before Alexander I', in G.W.S. Barrow, ed., *The Scottish Tradition*, Edinburgh.

Anderson, M.O. 1980, *Kings and Kingship in Early Scotland* (revised edition) Edinburgh.

Anderson, M.O. 1982, 'Dalriada and the creation of the Kingdom of the Scots', in Dumville, et al., 106-32.

Bannerman, John 1993, '*Comarba Coluim Chille* and the Relics of Columba', *Innes Review* 44, 14-47.

Best, R.I., and Lawlor, H.J., eds 1931, *The Martyrology of Tallaght* (Henry Bradshaw Society, vol.68) London.

Blair, J. and Sharpe, R., eds 1992, *Pastoral Care Before the Parish*, Leicester.

Breatnach, Liam 1989, 'The first third of *Bretha Nemed Toísech*', *Ériu* 40, 1-40.

Broun, Dauvit 1994, 'The origin of Scottish identity in its European context', in Crawford, 21-31.

Charles-Edwards, T.M. 1992, 'The pastoral role of the church in the early Irish laws', in Blair and Sharpe, 110-33.

Clancy, Thomas Owen and Márkus, Gilbert 1995, *Iona: the earliest poetry of a Celtic monastery*, Edinburgh.

Crawford, Barbara E., ed. 1994, *Scotland in Dark Age Europe*, St Andrews.

Dumville, D., McKitterick, R. and Whitelock, D. 1982, *Ireland in Early Medieval Europe*, Cambridge.

Etchingham, Colmán 1991, 'The early Irish church: some observations on pastoral care and dues', *Ériu* 42, 139-62.

Etchingham, Colmán 1993, 'The implications of *paruchia* ', *Ériu* 44, 139-62.

Etchingham, Colmán 1994, 'Bishops in the early Irish church: a re-assessment', *Studia Hibernica* (forthcoming).

Forbes, A.P. 1872, *Kalendars of Scottish Saints*, Edinburgh.

Forsyth, Katherine 1995, 'The Inscriptions on the Dupplin Cross', *From the Isles of the North: Medieval Art in Ireland and Britain* (Proceedings of the Third International Conference on Insular Art, Belfast, April 1994), Belfast.

Henderson, Isabel 1967, *The Picts*. London.

Herbert, Máire 1988, *Iona, Kells and Derry: The History and Hagiography of the Monastic* Familia *of Columba*, Oxford.

Herbert, Máire 1994, 'Charter material from Kells', in F. O'Mahony, *The Book of Kells: Proceedings of a conference at Trinity College Dublin, 6-9 September 1992*, Cambridge.

Hudson, Benjamin T. 1994, 'Kings and Church in Early Scotland', *Scottish Historical Review* 73, 145-70.

Hughes, Kathleen 1966, *The Church in Early Irish Society*, Ithaca, NY.

Kelleher, John 1971, 'The *Táin* and the annals', *Ériu* 22, 107-27.

Kenney, James F. 1929, *The Sources for the Early History of Ireland: Ecclesiastical*, New York.

Jackson, Kenneth 1972, *The Gaelic Notes in the Book of Deer*, Cambridge.

MacQuarrie, Alan 1992, 'Early Christian religious houses in Scotland: foundation and function', in Blair and Sharpe, 110-33.

Meyer, Kuno 1906, 'Regula Mucuta Raithni', in W. Stokes and K. Meyer, eds, *Archiv für celtische Lexicographie*, Halle.

Miller, Molly 1982, 'Matriliny by treaty: the Pictish foundation-legend', in Dumville et al., 133-61.

O' Dwyer, P. 1981, *Céli Dé: Spiritual reform in Ireland 750-900*, Dublin.

O' Keeffe, J.G. 1904, 'The Rule of Patrick', *Ériu* 1, 216-24.

Ó Riain, Pádraig P. 1990, 'The Tallaght Martyrologies, redated', *Cambridge Medieval Celtic Studies* 20, 21-38.

Reeves, William 1864, *On the Céli-Dé, commonly called Culdees*. (originally RIA Transactions xxiv).

Sharpe, Richard 1984, 'Some problems concerning the organization of the church in early medieval Ireland', *Peritia* 3, 230-70.

Sharpe, Richard 1992, 'Churches and communities in early medieval Ireland: towards a pastoral model', in Blair and Sharpe, 110-33.

Smyth, Alfred 1984, *Warlords and Holy Men: Scotland AD 80-1000*, London.

Wasserschleben, Hermann 1885, *Die Irische Kanonensammlung*, Lepizig.

CHAPTER 7

The Emergence of the *Regnum Scottorum*: a Carolingian hegemony?

Patrick Wormald

The first, central and I hope abiding message of this paper, all else that follows notwithstanding, is that we do not know how the kingdom of the Scots came into being, and we never shall. It was one of the two formative political developments of early medieval British history. It happened at more or less the same time as the other, the Making of England. Unlike the Making of England (though, as I shall stress, not *so very* unlike), it can also be called the last major development of British prehistory. It was the last time that there was a significant change in the political and cultural contours of the British Isles without our being able to say much about how, let alone why. The Emergence of the *Regnum Scottorum* is, then, an object lesson in the frustrations of life as an early medieval historian. At the same time, a subtext of my paper, addressed to any prehistorians whom it may concern, is that the current vogue for denying that there ever was disruptive change (apart from internal social revolution), until the existence of written sources obliges us to admit as much, is overdue for reconsideration.[1]

What do historians do when confronted with what amounts to a wall of silence (or, at best, a burble of distant and indistinct voices)? One thing they can do is what Anglo-Saxon historians did until lately with their equivalent problem, which is not the emergence of *'Engla Lond'* but the transformation of lowland Britain between the early fifth and late sixth centuries. Each shard of surviving evidence is seized and crammed into its place in an interpretative vessel so crafted as to accommodate them all. The problem with this approach is that the value of evidence does not, unlike that of other commodities, actually increase with its scarcity. Material may come to assume for historians a significance quite other than that which it had for its authors: for example, we now tend to see the pre-conversion annals of the *Anglo-Saxon Chronicle* not as a record of the conquest of southern England in the sixth century, but as some sort of explanation and legitimation of the way it was ruled in the ninth. The difficulty may be enhanced when handling the products of Celtic culture, with its inclination to be not so much economical as inflationary with the truth (a far more grievous sin in the canon of our current masters); and with its positive genius for the manipulation of the regnal records which were part of its stock-in-trade. One of the blessings of being a Scottish early medievalist must be the legacy of Skene and Anderson: everything you need to know is brought miraculously within the compass of one binding. But it is apt to have the effect of reducing all sources to a common level of acceptability or otherwise; of playing down or overlooking the extent to which various texts may have varying slants - may even, if pulled apart and examined as wholes, be trying to say opposite things.

Another approach is that currently favoured by prehistorians, by some students of the *Adventus Saxonum,* and now by some interpreters of the Making of a Scottish kingdom: denial that anything very dramatic happened at all. The hints at continuity that the sources certainly offer are taken to preclude the sort of violent takeover that the same sources emphatically do not rule out. A pervasive view over the past quarter century sees the ground for Kenneth mac Alpin's ascendancy as prepared by two hundred and fifty years of a creeping 'Scotticization', above all through the impact of the Columban Church, but also through the gradual replacement of Pictish matrilineal regnal inheritance by Gaelic norms (Bannerman, 1971, 79; Anderson, 1982, 108-15).[2] I have to say right at the start that this line of thought is in my view open to one grave if not insuperable objection, namely the fate of the Pictish language. As I understand such things, Pictish was a P-Celtic tongue, so a lot more like Welsh than Gaelic (Forsyth, 1995a, further to Jackson, 1955, and Smyth, 1984, 46-52). I take this to mean that Gaelic and Pictish were no more mutually intelligible than Welsh and Irish, whose membership of a single linguistic family was undetected until the sixteenth century. There is no question of assimilation of Pictish into Gaelic. Nor has much evidence of significant Pictish substrata in Gaelic (yet) been unearthed (but cf. Greene, 1972, 1983; Macaulay, 1975). The linguistic pattern seems closer to that produced by the Anglo-Saxon than the Roman, Norse or Norman Conquests.

Now, prehistorians and others presently disinclined to credit the movement of large bodies of people across the map at any stage of the human experience are given to the nostrums that we do not know why or how languages change, and that physical removal is far from the only available explanation. This is true. It is also true that enforced domination, accompanied by some degree of migration, is a more obvious explanation than most, unless there are sound reasons to override it. The very latest account of the rise of the Scottish kingdom repudiates the taste of earlier generations of scholars for 'empire-building with battles', and goes so far as to call it 'a process that extended over a long period of time, (which) may have provoked so little notice because it was so unremarkable' (Hudson, 1994, 34-6, etc.). I fear it may symptomatize this interpretation that, for all that I can see, it is not once mentioned that Picts and Scots spoke different languages, or that the former's would become extinct.[3] No one today is going to elide the processes of political and linguistic change. No one, I presume, now supposes that Pictish was eliminated at once, or by 'ethnic cleansing' - though the phrase reminds us, as Patrick Sims-Williams and Tom Shippey recently observed in the *TLS,* that these things do happen. What seems inconceivable is that it could have been eclipsed, in the short or long term, without displacement of the elite that spoke it. We might fairly wonder whether a culture whose art (at least on one reading of its symbols: Thomas, 1961, 1963; Henderson, 1967, 115-60) shows every sign of vigorous attachment to a broadly indigenous repertoire, is likely to have lamely abandoned its speech.

As we leave that matter for the time being, there is one obvious proviso to be entered. I am making my case in a language that was not imposed upon these parts by force. Scotland from the twelfth century is a conspicuous example of a society which, mysteriously yet beyond serious cavil voluntarily, exchanged its ancestral tongue for that of a neighbour who was not always affectionately regarded. But before we are tempted to extrapolate from twelfth century circumstances to those of the ninth, there are two other points to bear in mind. For one thing, the activity of the French-speaking nobles and English hangers-on who provided the vehicle for lingustic and cultural change was of course anything but peaceful elsewhere (Davies, 1990; Frame, 1990). The context, that is to say, was one of violence, even if Scots were spared its manifestations to an extent that Welsh and Irish were not. Secondly, the twelfth century saw massive cultural change in the West as a whole. Professor Robert Bartlett's remarkable recent book (1993) illuminates as never before the ways in which 'minority' cultures channelled into the European mainstream, at times because they had to, but also on occasion from choice. There is no counterpart to such processes in the 'Barbarian West': among my messages in this paper is that the Carolingian 'Renaissance' meant not what that of the twelfth century meant for the Mecklenberg Slavs, to whom Bartlett compares the Scots, but the experience of ninth century Saxons - an experience that incidentally had among its side-effects the early medieval West's other proverbial vanishing act, that of the

once mighty Avars. Twenty-five years study of the Barbarian West's warrior aristocracies has yet to acquaint me with one that rolled over and died of osmosis.

If we cannot solve the problem of Scotland's emergence merely by piecing bits together or even by pretending that there is no problem to solve, what *are* we to do? The answer of course is, to guess. But we can and should control our guesswork by doing what three admirable papers did at the last 'Dark Age Scotland' symposium within these walls (Crawford, 1994): that is, to examine the pattern of comparable developments in parts of the West whose documentation is not so exiguous. Rather than read back in time from the known to the unknown, the method patented by Maitland's classic *Domesday Book and Beyond* (1897), we can read across in place from the brightly lit to the dimly visible. Hence, I can make clear at this point that most (not all) of what I mean by a 'Carolingian hegemony' is the kind of statecraft being practised elsewhere in the contemporary West. Can we perceive a shape to events in other eighth/ninth century kingdoms that would make sense of what little we can see of the Scots?

The first theme that I want to pick out is precisely the apparent continuity that so dominates current perceptions of the subject. It is in fact the message of the early parts of the Table (below pp.148-50), which aims to marshal all the main evidence bearing on the issue. If the eye of faith is up to penetrating the mysteries of material where, as Professor Duncan once remarked, 'rationality departs from our sources' (Duncan, 1975, 54), col. 4 will show that Dál Riatan tradition as reflected in eleventh century sources, and Pictish records as mediated by the Picto-Scottish king-lists in the reign of Malcolm III, were together maintaining that Picts and Scots had three or four kings in common through the half century to 839: perhaps a Conall, certainly a Constantine son of Fergus, an Angus son of Fergus and an Eoganan son of Angus. All these kings appear in the one contemporary source, the *Annals of Ulster*, where the first is found fighting 'among the Picts' but being killed 'in Kintyre', while the other three are kings neither of Dál Riata nor of the Picts but 'of Fortriu'.[4] Just to complicate matters, however, there are contemporaneous Dál Riatan kings who are not in Pictish lists: Domnall and/or Donncorci and Aed mac Boanta; and *vice versa:* Drest son of Constantine, and Talorgan (merged in the 'Q' tradition), then Ferat, Bridei and another trio confined to the 'Q' list, which ends with a Drest killed at Forteviot or Scone.

This tableau has naturally attracted a deal of skilled remoulding and realignment, notably from the deft hands of Marjorie Anderson and the vigorous grip of Benjamin Hudson. Approaches tend to fall into two lines of thought. The first takes the kings the two traditions share as essentially Picts (Skene, 1876, I, 301-16; Duncan, 1975, 54-9; and (with modifications) Anderson, 1982, 108-15). They may well have had Dál Riatan fathers, as Pictish matriliny would allow; if so, they were indeed legitimate heirs to each throne, so that a relatively peaceful union of Pict and Scot would be feasible in terms of either's values. Still, inherent in this scheme is a degree of Pictish domination over Scots, in that Constantine was apparently king of the former well before he ruled the latter. On this view, the role of Kenneth mac Alpin was to turn the tables on the Pictish masters, while exploiting the climate of subjection to a single monarch that they had fostered. The other interpretation (Chadwick, 1949, 127-33; Smyth, 1984, 177-85; Hudson, 1994, 29-33) plays down any Pictish matrilineal factor (anyway in retreat in so far as Drest and Eoganan at least were sons of kings), and sees Constantine and company as Scots.[5] They are thus harbingers of Kenneth's triumph; for Hudson, it is in fact they, not Kenneth, who deserve the palm of conquerors of Pictland. All that Kenneth did was secure their throne for his branch of the Dál Riatan dynasty; his family's ultimate monopoly of it was what ensured the immortality of his name instead of theirs (cf. Broun, 1994a, 22-3).

I do not propose to choose between these solutions to the puzzle. Part of its beauty is that they could both be right up to a point. To introduce two considerations brought into the debate by Katherine Forsyth's recent work. Her discovery that the inscription on the Dupplin Cross commemorates 'Custantin filius Fircus' (1995) would seem to favour a 'Scottish' *persona*, though only if it is still seen as a fundamentally post-Pictish monument, and if of course it was put up by him, not in his honour and memory.[6] On the other hand, her forthcoming paper on the 'Pictish' royal names in the Lindisfarne *Liber Vitae* shows that there is still a hint of Pictish orthography in its spelling of Uoenan's name, if not of Constantine's own; this therefore backs up the lesson of the survival of Pictish spelling in the king-lists down to the mid-century, the point made by Dauvit Broun (1994a, 22), and one further reinforced by the fact that Constantine seems to have given his son the decidedly Pictish name of Drest.

The point I wish to make is that, instead of trying to adjust the sources into a pattern that makes more sense of them, we should ask why they seem to be talking nonsense in the first place. Is it not on the cards that, when we deduce that the scene was set for Kenneth mac Alpin by his immediate predecessors one way or the other, *this was the very impression that the evidence is trying to give us?* Whatever the circumstances in which Kenneth's cousins (if they were his cousins) took power in Fortriu, it was certainly in his interest to stress that Pict and Scot could be represented as having had much the same rulers for the previous half-century. There are several reasons why surface appearances might prompt a 'double-take'. For one thing, the 'X'/'Y' lists have clearly been tampered with, so as to secure the royal title of Kenneth's father, and such lightning could strike more than once. The disqualification of this record leaves only the 'Synchronisms' and *Duan* as evidence that Constantine, Angus and Eoganan ever were kings of Scots as well as Picts; it is not certain that they represent two witnesses rather than one; and even if they do, information relayed to Ireland by an eleventh century Scottish establishment should not be regarded as foolproof.[7] In any case, the several signs of garbling in these sources' sequences just before Kenneth (Table, n. (iv)) are consistent with an undercooked tradition.[8]

In addition, much of the remaining evidence is at pains to uphold a 'continuity' thesis. Even the most 'Pictish' king-lists ('P') reach us only as continued by lists of their Scottish successors. At the eleventh century stage conveyed by the 'B' and and 'C' lists, there is no hint of a break at Kenneth (col. 4); and though the *Synchronisms* make the remark quoted there, nothing portentous is said by the solidly Gaelic *Duan Albanach* either (col. 4). As Mrs Anderson has pointed out (1973, 78-9), it looks as though the 'B'/'C' list once terminated not with 'et Bred' but with 'et Custantin fil. Cinæda': in other words, it ran on uninterrupted for the first three Scottish kings, crossing the critical gulf of a new generation. And although list 'A' cuts off in favour of a chronicle with a rather different burden (col. 2), as we shall see, several scholars have noted (most recently, Broun, 1994b, 40-5) that 'Pictish' terminology stays consistently in place all down col. 2 until 900, before at last giving way to 'Albania'. Just to show that this is no chance, exactly the same feature is found in col. 1, the strictly contemporary *Annals of Ulster*, with whose compilers, as Hudson persuasively suggests (1994, 55), it is a fair guess that Kenneth's spokesmen had their contacts.

All this is to say, then, that we cannot decide for sure who truly engineered the Scottish takeover of Pictland. Equally, we are scarcely entitled to reject the

dominant version relayed by our sources merely because other texts tell a story that may be every bit as artificial. On the whole, it remains somewhat easier to believe that Kenneth played upon the precedent of residually 'Scottish' royal Picts than that Scottish forerunners were skilfully reprogrammed as pseudo-Picts.[9] In any event, it was the careful spatchcocking of the two traditions that has made the whole issue impenetrable. Continuity was at a premium. In the early medieval West it very often was.

Here, my parallels from elsewhere in Britain and Europe first come in. The most glaring case of the use and abuse of continuity is the rise, a century and a half later, of Brian Bóruma (Byrne, 1973, 11). He began as ruler of the Dál Cais, a petty dynasty from County Clare (like another family of moment in Irish history, the de Valeras). He ended as *imperator Scottorum*, as his secretary wrote in the venerable Book of Armagh. Along the way he was genealogically linked to the Eóganachta, Munster's traditional rulers. The link is patently false - patently, because of the unrivalled richness of the Irish genealogical record. But it conveyed a political truth, which is what mattered. Again, at much the same time as Scots were gaining power in Pictland, the dynasty of Merfyn began its spectacular ascent by seizing the throne of Gwynedd (Davies, 1982a, 105-7). Rhodri Mawr, his son, took over Ceredigion and Powys, while Hywel Dda, his great-grandson, swallowed Dyfed. Each move was legitimized by inter-marriage and descent in the female line. That apart, the scenario was lent a certain familiarity by putting about a story of how another warlord had come to power in Gwynedd four centuries before, naming its sub-kingdoms after the sons to which he assigned them. The story of Cunedda was good enough to fool all historians before David Dumville (1977b, 181-3). On more familiar West Saxon ground, Ecgberht, King Alfred's grandfather, claimed rule of both Wessex and Kent by family right (Scharer, 1996). He may have been justified in either respect; hardly however in both. Last come the Carolingians themselves, arch-exponents of the 'consensus *putsch*'. Merovingian blood had turned up in their veins by the ninth century; well before that, Charlemagne gave the names of his greatest predecessors to two legitimate sons and one bastard (Wallace-Hadrill, 1971, 106). It is hard to say who was really taken in by all this. It may be wrong to ask. The rhetoric of familiarity met a deeply felt demand. Elites never far from the threshold of brutal violence needed to sense that their politics had its formal aspect. Sources lie, those for ninth century Scotland most probably included; they lie because in a way they were expected to.[10]

And so we come to my second theme: violence. In this instance, it may help to begin with the wider scene, a short discourse on the use of force in the early medieval West. I suspect that, as English-speakers, we are at a disadvantage here from the domination of our consciousness by the most notorious of all medieval conquests. Yet Hastings was one of extremely few politically decisive battles between Adrianople and Bouvines. When Charlemagne marched on Lombardy in 774, opposition expired with barely token resistance. Lombard institutions were in general respected; but one has to search quite hard among the ranks of those running them under Frankish rule to find a scion of the old Lombard aristocracy (Wickham, 1981, 48, 73-4). When the Avars were wiped off the map by a brilliantly coordinated campaign, violence was apparently limited to the overrunning of their great 'Ring' or stockade; and it was the distribution throughout Europe of the hoard of treasure they had accumulated over centuries that signalled the evaporation of their power (Pohl, 1988, 312-23). In an age when armies (or the effective parts of them) fought for plunder not pay, the enemy's treasury was the prime military target (Reuter, 1985, 1990); the richer it was, the further it went towards erecting a substitute lordship.

Moving to Britain, West Saxon kings fought no battles between 910 and 937 when establishing an ascendancy over what became England; it is a point of some relevance to us that much of the course of these blistering campaigns would be wholly unknown, but for the survival of a lone text of the *Anglo-Saxon Chronicle* (Whitelock, 1979, 213-18). One piece of evidence, however - just one and surviving once more by the merest chance - reveals that those who did not come instantly to terms with the march of Edward the Elder's army forfeited their lands *ipso facto* (Blake, 1962, 98-9). If we return to the Gwynedd dynasty, the Scots' closest contemporary counterparts, we find few battles marking their progress in either the Welsh Annals or Asser (Morris, 1980, 48-9, 89-91; Keynes and Lapidge, 1983, 94-6): feeble authorities maybe, but a significant improvement upon anything from Scotland. The last thing that we are therefore entitled to conclude from the failure of ninth century Scottish sources to give plausible accounts of military encounters is that Scottish control was basically achieved peacefully. It may not even be wrong to rule out of all consideration the later legends - already known to Berchan, col. 3 - of dirty tricks at the Scone dinner table. Peter Heather reminded this assembly two years ago that abuse of hospitality was a standard tactic in Roman or tenth century German handling of obtrusive neighbours (1994, 60).

What Kenneth mac Alpin (or Constantine mac Fergus) would have had to do to establish their supremacy, if Charlemagne's pulverization of the Saxons is anything to go by, was to sustain an unusually persistent version of what the Irish Annals almost annually characterize as a 'hosting'. Keeping up the pressure across Scotland's central belt and beyond, targeting fort after fort, rewarding submission and disposing ruthlessly of the recalcitrant, would in the end demoralize Pictish opposition as it did others exposed to similar strategies. But do we have grounds to think the Scots capable of such campaigning? Two years ago, Dauvit Broun thought that possibly 'there was not much left of Dál Riata after a couple of decades of Norse settlement in the Western Isles and Western sea-board' (1994a, 22). I think it possible that the truth may in a sense be the opposite of this. I hasten to say that I accept Dr Hudson's elegant removal from the stage of nearly all props that have lent verisimilitude to the image of Viking rulers as collaborators with the Scots (1994, 40-2, 46, 89, etc.). What gives me pause about his going on to argue that they were the enemy of Scottish expansion and vigorously combatted, as constantly stressed by our nearest to a reliable record, the 'Poppleton' Chronicle (col. 2), is once again comparison with Wales and Ireland.

With Brian Bóruma, we are as usual on well-charted ground. Until quite recent times, Irish histories still celebrated Brian as the hero of a national crusade against the Vikings. We now know that the reason this seemed so true for so long was that his dynasty put out a telling piece of propaganda to that effect: the 'War of the Gaedhil and the Gaill (Irish and *Foreigners*)' (Todd, 1867). As a matter of fact, Brian owed much of his success to an ability to milk the fleets, levies and revenues of Viking towns under his sway (Ó'Corráin, 1972, 120-31). Further to that, Professor Wendy Davies has adduced the high probability of Viking participation in the vicissitudes of Gwynedd politics from the second half of the tenth century (Davies, 1990, 56-60). Thomas Charles-Edwards now draws my attention to (late) evidence that the dynasty of Merfyn itself came from the Isle of Man (Charles-Edwards, 1995, 706-7). If this is right, it may have a real bearing on how we think about the shape of things further north in the west British archipelago: in 'Sodor (Dál Riata)' (his phrase) as opposed to Man. From the first appearance of Norse freebooters in the 'Irish Sea province', a reservoir of military energy began to build up, its power at the disposal of any warlord who found promising channels for its outflow. The triumph of the Scots might then be a first manifestation in British history of the formidable punch packed until early modern times by the Lordship of the Isles.

Judging by the Irish parallel, the Poppleton Chronicle's impression of an epic struggle with Vikings should not be allowed to exclude the possibility. In this connection, two final observations can be made. First, Scots knew from the start what King Alfred had to learn from experience: the value when dealing with Vikings of ships. In the seventh century, the muster of the *fer nAlban* was already in part naval (Bannerman, 1974, 43, 49). Second, the overall effect of Vikings in the British sphere and beyond was up to a point to recreate the hectic conditions of the immediately post-Roman 'Heroic Age'. As well as furnishing recruits for warbands, they unleashed new supplies of the treasure that fused warbands together, by liquefying so much of the precious metal that had been cast into church plate over the previous four centuries. The Scots may have been among the beneficiaries of a markedly destabilized ninth century scene - whether or not they were among the few who rode the Viking tiger without ending up inside it.[11]

My third theme does concern more peaceful aspects of the exercise of early medieval hegemony; or rather, an ideology which could be as merciless in its application and as devastating in its effects as any hosting. We can begin with legislation. It hardly needs saying today that the making of law (whatever this actually amounted to) was seen by the Carolingians as an integral part of their *via regia*. Just as well known is that Alfred's dynasty signalled its new political and governmental consciousness by a more or less sustained legislative programme, launched by a lawbook of Alfred's own which was essentially a restatement of his people's law within a new ideological framework (Wormald, 1977, 128-32). More directly relevant in understanding the Mac Alpins is that there is reason to think that Celtic kings were affected by this trend, though their efforts survive barely if at all. So Brian Bóruma is said by the *Annals of Inisfallen* to have taken hostages 'as a guarantee of the banishment of robbers and the lawless' (Mac Airt, 1951, 167). The Annals show his successors making laws (*cána*) against theft (Ó'Corráin, 1974, 22-4). Only the Annals let us know this, because that sort of law was not kept among the voluminous memorials of early Irish jurisprudence. The situation in Wales is yet more intriguing. Welsh lawbooks from the high Middle Ages all stand in the name of Hywel Dda, the most powerful king of the tenth century. This is not merely a matter of a predictably bogus prologue. Hywel's intervention is signalled often enough throughout the texts themselves to leave little doubt that he or his authority had once played a major role in the process (Jenkins, 1986, 1, 52, 94, 110, etc.). Yet Welsh law comes out like Irish, as lawyers' tracts. Not one enunciation can be confidently ascribed to Hywel. In this light, it seems entirely credible that, as Stuart Airlie stressed last time around (1994, 34-6), Donald I marked his dynasty's new eminence by a great legislative jamboree (col. 2), reissuing the law of a Dál Riatan predecessor; it is certainly not to be disbelieved in overreaction to the musings of Fordun or even later 'authorities' (Haddan and Stubbs, 1878, 122-4(!); Duncan, 1993; Anderson, 1982, 122-3; Wormald, 1986, 168-9).

One sort of characteristically Celtic lawgiving may be especially important. Here, it is best to begin by standing back, for one last time, in search of the widest possible vision. In early medieval political discourse, 'reform' was the other side of the 'continuity' coin. It was naturally the one that was uppermost more often as the passage of time made it less necessary to stress the lack of change. But that does not mean that it was not focal for the self-image of new regimes from their inception. It is of course a much more palpable Carolingian theme than continuity (Ullmann, 1969; McKitterick, 1977). Carolingians never forgot - were never allowed to forget - that they owed their crown to the sanction of the Pope and of a Church who looked to them for Josiah-like redress of the unregeneracy that had so angered God as to unleash the forces of Islam. With the West Saxons, it all began at a humbler level. But the 838/9 deal which set up the succession (and most probably unction) of Ecgberht's son Æthelwulf, the first father-son succession in Wessex for two centuries, involved concessions to Canterbury and probably Winchester (Brooks, 1984, 197-203). By the eleventh century, Archbishop Wulfstan was outpacing the Carolingians themselves in his zeal for an ordered and holy society. It would be hard to find such active concern in Celtic kings. Still, Irish rulers were induced to grant exemptions to churches general and specific from the various burdens of secular government; so Áed 'the Ordained' was persuaded in 804 by a synod under the Abbot of Armagh to free churches from supplying recruits for his 'hosting'; and Brian in 1012 freed 'all St Patrick's churches' from secular imposts (Byrne, 1973, 159-60; Ó'Corráin, 1972, 127; Ó'Riáin, 1990). That policy at least was of a piece with Europe-wide awareness of the value to kings of cultivating the goodwill of saints, above all those who were in any sense 'national' saints. Carolingians adopted the 'special patronage' of St Denis. Æthelwulf lavishly re-adorned the shrine of Aldhelm, the West Saxon royal saint and scholar (Hamilton, 1870, 389-90); his later successors earnestly solicited the support of St Cuthberht for their northern strategy (Rollason, 1989, 144-52). Brian was rewarded for his services to St Patrick with the unparalleled honour (for a non-Uí Néill layman) of burial at Armagh (Byrne, 1973, 256-7). Even in Wales, the poet/prophet of *Armes Prydein* looked to the intercession of 'Dewi and the saints of Britain' to put 'the foreigners' (English) to flight (Williams, 1982, 4-5, 8-9). Carolingian and sub-Carolingian kings all had a *Kirchenpolitik.* It was their duty and their interest.

The relevance of all this for the earliest Scottish kings emerges from excerpts in the Table. It is part of a distinct if subtle shift of emphasis as between the twelfth century ('X'/'Q') records in col. 5 and the eleventh century evidence of col. 4 that more is made of a new deal for the Church (though not without finding suitable precedents, as when the foundation of the nodal shrines of Dunkeld and St Andrews is credited to the key figures of Constantine and Angus, sons of Fergus). Thus, Giric 'first gave freedom to the Scottish Church which was under servitude until that time after the custom and manner of the Picts'. It is reasonable to connect this with the freedoms granted by Irish kings (Cowan, 1981, 11), but with the critical rider that *a new dispensation is this time linked to a drastic change of secular regime.* The standing of the twelfth century records is unfortunately far from secure. But Giric's contribution is startlingly borne out by the mysterious 'Dunkeld litany' (Table, *ad fin.*), with its very Carolingian invocation for 'his army'. The 'reform' theme also comes out clearly in a much better source, the Poppleton Chronicle (col. 2). Though even this can be no earlier as it stands than the 970s, it may, to repeat, be wrong to regard it as purely retrospective justification for change that was in reality much smoother. The themes of 'Reform' and 'Continuity' were complementary in images of Carolingian and post-1066 change; and each is in different ways stressed by the Poppleton Chronicle itself. Thus it may well say something significant about the spirit in which the Scottish takeover was conceived from its very outset that it includes a counterpart to Giric's concession, though ascribed to Constantine II and his bishop. Even more suggestive is a passage whose seminal importance was spotted by Ted Cowan (1981, 14): 'God deemed (Picts) deserving of being deprived of their inheritance by reason of their wickedness, because they not only spurned the mass and commandment of the Lord, but in right of justice would not be put on a level with others'. It does not matter what (if anything) the Picts had actually done wrong. Here is the hiss of the most lethal weapon in the early medieval ideologue's arsenal: the image of a people expelled for its sins from its promised land.

I have recently argued that Bede and Alfred provided the ideological charter of a new English kingdom by adapting the Israelite model to Anglo-Saxon experience of the Britons and the Vikings (1994). And yes, I now venture the same proposal for the Scots, their compeers in ninth century statecraft. The history of the Scots diverged from that of their fellow-Celts at this point, with all that that was to mean for the future of these islands, because they did what the Welsh or Irish never quite managed to do: they harnessed a compelling political idea. They could represent themselves as instruments of God's wrath at the sort of backslidings which, in Gildas view as rehearsed by Bede, had once cost Britons their homeland and would now exact the same cruel price from Picts. But the Scottish picture has an intriguing twist. The role provided for a patron saint was in this case so central as to make Denis, Patrick or David seem peripheral. Archie Duncan proposed at length and with force (1981) that, whether or not Columba was the Apostle of the Picts, the Picts themselves believed as much by the time they got in touch with Monkwearmouth-Jarrow over the Easter issue. But Columba was a Scot, not a Pict; he was above all a patron of Dál Riata. What was more, the Picts had ignominiously sent his clergy packing back in 717. So Scots could also portray themselves as the agents of his irate return. And that is just what they did. One of the Poppleton Chronicle's rare snippets on Kenneth (col. 2) is his translation of Columba's relics to a church he built, probably Dunkeld. Stuart Airlie has eloquently expounded the logic of such moves (1994, 36-41). Alan MacQuarrie (1992, 122-3) notes the implications of a Dunkeld cross-slab, replete with martial imagery ('exercitu suo'), and with echoes of Columban reformist sculpture in Ireland. Meanwhile, a non-ecclesiastical perspective is given by col. 3. Amidst all Berchan's gobbledygook, one message comes over loud and clear. Kenneth and his successors are treading where Columba (and Áedan mac Gabráin) had trodden before. A saint comes unto his own. This time, they have no choice but to receive him.[12]

Thomas Clancy's discoveries about Abbot Diarmait of Iona confirm my long-held suspicion that more might be unearthed along these lines by study of the mind-set of the *Céli De* reform. If the persistence of the word means anything, it may have had yet more influence in ninth century Scotland than in Ireland.[13] There, according to Francis-John Byrne (1973, 157-8), it propagated ideals of Carolingian kingship. Dr Clancy's argument speaks for itself. I shall conclude by returning more or less to where we started. By the second half of the ninth century, the idiom of Irish churchmanship was substantially, even aggressively, vernacular; this may be especially true of the *Céli De* (e.g.

Kenney, 1929, 468-82). Now, when rightly insisting at the 1993 symposium that analysis of ninth century Scotland had to reckon with the disappearance of Pictish, Dauvit Broun proposed the disruption of traditional social structures caused by the Vikings as a possible factor (1994a, 27-30). The difficulty here is that it is not obvious why the Vikings (or even any 'social change' arising) should have been so much more subversive of Pictish Ps than of Gaelic Qs. However, if the Scottish conquest were bound up with the strident assertiveness of a reforming and emphatically Gaeliphone Church, then it is possible to see how Pictish could be marginalized. A new ethnicity would coalesce around the tongue in which Columba entertained his string of angelic guests. It may not be chance that Constantine II was the hero, after Kenneth, of Berchan as well as the chronicles: just in the time of this would-be *Céli De* abbot, we begin to hear of *Alba*. Against that setting, the displacement of Gaelic culture from the Scottish establishment after the twelfth century would create the semi-prehistoric mists though which we must all peer. It is one good answer to Kathleen Hughes's question, 'Where are the writings of early Scotland?' (1980), that many were lost when Gaelic, like Columba, went out of fashion. And by the time that Scots were again preoccupied with a literate vernacular, it was not, very much not, the one they had spoken half a millenium before; there was thus no place for a Scottish Archbishop Matthew Parker.

Over the last two decades, I have been learning that extrapolating from England's history is not necessarily the best way to understand Scotland's. For all that, I am prepared to say that aspects of '1066 And All That' may not take us too far from what happened in 842. Like the Normans or the West Saxons and Carolingians before, Scots could claim a legitimate title to Pictland from recent political history. Like them, they could seem to create a climate under which the Church might live in a new freedom; and if we can envisage the Carolingian or Lanfrancian reforms powered by a far more self-confident vernacular than Alfred's or Wulfstan's English ever was, we may get some way towards realizing their impact. In any event, just because we know so little about him is no excuse for denying Kenneth mac Alpin the role of conqueror assigned to better documented 'Dark Age' hegemonists. It is what the record does ultimately invite us to do. I am ready to say, then, that the Picts were after all conquered by the Scots in the ninth century. Their aristocracy suffered in the same way as others, the English of 1066 not least, from the advent of rulers prepared to stress all forms of continuity except the *locus* of the incumbent elite (place-names with 'Pit-' prefixes to Gaelic personal names always seem to me

to speak volumes); rulers who simultaneously or soon came to see their role as the scourge of God on a corrupt ecclesiastical establishment in the name of the saint who first brought the Faith to North Britain. Guesswork? Well, yes. But guesswork which predicates nothing for Scotland's history not attested for similar societies under comparable conditions. And guesswork which, whatever its other faults, does have the merit of imagining that the first Celtic culture to die out in these islands did not do so without a fight.

Christ Church
University of Oxford

Notes ~~~~~~

The Emergence of the Regnum Scottorum

1. This foray into what has been wisely described as 'one of those refreshing issues about which complete agreement is impossible' (Broun, 1994a, 21), is inspired by the experience of fifteen years' teaching at the University of Glasgow and attendance at the 'Scottish Medievalists'; in particular, to what I learned from working with Professors Archie Duncan and Leslie Alcock; and, more crucially if more obviously, to a life shared with a third distinguished historian of Scotland. Apart from those general debts, I am most grateful to Katherine Forsyth for generously sharing her already almost unrivalled knowledge of Pictish problems, and for further advice to Dauvit Broun, Thomas Charles-Edwards, Roger Collins, Rees Davies and Archie Duncan. However, it follows from Dr Broun's *caveat* that none of these scholars is answerable for my paper's lingering perversities. I say little of archaeology, art-history or place-names: not only are they covered by other essays in this series, but I am even less equipped to dabble in such depths than in the eddies of the written sources; the parameters of artefactual and linguistic research have anyway tended to be set by understanding of more 'purely' historical evidence. In the text, though not when it matters in the table, I have usually anglicized the spelling of Celtic names, so as to retain an element of recognition in what is already regrettably rebarbative.

2. The pioneer of this approach to the problem seems in fact to have been Watson, 1926, 218-34.

3. I would add that if Dr Hudson's book seems to attract more than its fair share of my critical attention, that is a tribute to his immensely stimulating treatment of the subject.

4. Too much should not, however, be made of the 'Fortriu' label in the early ninth century: it was used for such unimpeachably (and exclusively?) Pictish kingships as that of Bridei s. Bile (Mac Airt and Mac Niocaill, 1983, 154-5); and cf. *ibid.*, 216-17.

5. It will be evident that I accept the case for Pictish matriliny (Miller, 1982; Sellar, 1985), at least in so far as the change that seems to come over the Pictish king-lists in the ninth century is best explained in this way. However, the exploitation of *Lex Salica* in the fourteenth century by French lawyers bent on excluding the succession of Edward III serves as a reminder that such 'customs' can just as well be rooted in recent political pressures as in immemorial tradition.

6. Ms Forsyth tells me that she herself regards this as 'a *Pictish* monument from the opening decades of the ninth century'; this is what is indicated by the art-historical evidence, the use of Latin rather than Irish, and 'the very significant Anglo-Saxon artistic influence'. The general impression is that it is both 'eclectic' and 'up-to-date', 'an import from Gaeldom in the latest style'; 'The representation of a Pictish name (Fircus) in Gaelic orthography would fit in with this'. For another recent assessment, see Alcock (1992), 238-41.

7. As noted by Boyle (1971, 170), there are signs that the 'Synchronisms' were in some sense written with Scottish sensitivities in mind. By the same token, no other Irish source can easily be taken as confirmation of the 'truth' about the Dál Riatan ascendancy: Hudson, 1994, 30-1, 54-5; cf. his point cited below about Cenél nGabráin influence on *AU*, transmitted *via* the contacts that each had with the Uí Néill, among the implications of which is that the Irish Annals may conceal the element of violent disruption in the Scottish takeover.

8. This is not to say that Kenneth's own descent is fraudulent: he could perfectly well have been 'son of Alpin, son of Eochaid, son of Áed Finn, etc.', as claimed by the apparently tenth-century 'Genealogy of Alba' (Bannerman, 1974, 65-7), without Alpin ever having been an acknowledged king.

9. Perhaps the best case for Constantine's 'Scottishness' is a name which, if Alan Macquarrie is right (1990, 10-13), is likelier to have been given to a man schooled for Scottish rather than Pictish rule.

10. It is a drawback of Mrs Anderson's ground-breaking, scholarly, and often inherently plausible argumentation (1973, 1982, etc.) that it was conceived before the 'genealogical revolution' of the 1970s (best epitomized by Dumville, 1977a) made its effects felt.

11. This interpretation of conditions on the western seaboard has an obvious bearing on Dr Hudson's suggestion (1994, 56-7, 128-47) that the Cenél Loairn penetrated the Great Glen at much the same time as the Cenél nGabráin made their way into Strathmore, providing kings Giric and Constantine in the ninth century, and Macbeth and Lulach in the eleventh. The Macbeth and Lulach genealogies (O'Brien, 1962, 329-30) may very well not be authentic, while that of Giric is as late as Fordun. But contemporary assaults by freebooting bands on the north-east seem entirely likely, whether or not under Cenél Loairn auspices.

12. For the use of Columba's relics in battle, see Airlie (1994), 37-41; Hudson (1994), 70; and cf. Smyth (1984), 213-14. Whether or not it is true that the dynasty were usually buried on Iona (Cowan, 1981, 7), it is a fact that four of its members were named 'servant of the Dove/Columba'; and Máel Coluim was not a common name among the legion of Irish kings. As late as the first quarter of the twelfth century, Alexander I apparently commissioned a copy of Adomnan from an 'insula pontificum' (probably *Céli De* Loch Leven): Anderson, 1961, 10.

13. One result of Dr Clancy's research is to remove some of the reservations about use of the term *Céli De* in twelfth century contexts that were powerfully urged by the late Professor Ian Cowan (1974).

Tabulated Evidence ~~~~~~~~~~~~~~~~~~~~~~~~~~~~~~~~~

The Emergence of the Regnum Scottorum

I Annals of Ulster	II Poppleton Chronicle	III Berchan	IV King-lists Synchr./Duan/P	V King-lists X/Q
781 Death of Fergus m. Ecach (= Eochaid) 'ri Dal Riati'		([Columba] will be a scholar, a seer, a sage of the son of God ... a warrior and cleric, pure and fierce ... ... He will not be absent in Iona (though he come to Ireland) ... [Áedan m. Gabráin] will cast the Picts into insignificance He is the first man who will rise in the East ... ...)	*(Fergus <f.> Eochoidh)*	*Fergus f. Hethfin* *[Sealuhanc]* *[Heoghed]* *[Dungal]* *[Alpin f. Heoghed]*
782 Death of Dub Tholarg 'rex Pictorum citra Monoth'	[Talorgen f. Onuist]		Talorcen f. Oinuist	Talargan f. Tenegus
789 'Bellum inter Pictos', Conall m. Tadc defeated, Constantine victor	[Canaul f. Tarl'a] [Castantin f. Wrguist]		Canaul f. Tang Caustantin f. Uurguist	Constantin f. Fergusa ... 'Hic ædificavit Dunkelden'
792 Death of 'Donn Corci rex Dal Riatai'			*Domnall (m. Cusantin)*	
807 Killing of Conall m. Tadc by Conall m. Aedacan 'in Cenn Tíre'			*Conall X 2* *Custaintin (m. Fergusa)*	
820 Death of 'Custantin m. Fergusa, rex Fortreinn'				
	[Unuist f. Wrguist]		Uidnuist f. Uurguist	Hungus f. Fergusa: ... 'Hic ædificavit Kilrymont'
834 Death of 'Oengus m. Fergusa, rex Fortrenn'	[Drest f. Constantini et Talorgen f. Wthoil]		*Aengus (m. Fergusa)* Drest f. Constantin et Talorc f. Uuthoil	Dustalorg
839 'Genntib' victory over 'men of Fortriu', death of Eoganan m. Oengus, Bran m. Oengus, Aed m. Boanta & 'almost innumerable'	[Uuen f. Unuist] [Wrad f. Bargoit] [... et Bred]		*Aedh (m. Boanta)* *Eoghanan (m. Oengusa)* Unen f. Unuist Uurad f. Bargoit ... et Bred *? Ailpin (m. Echach)*	Eoganan f. Hungus Ferat f. Batot Brude f. Ferat Kinat f. Ferat Brude f. Fotel Drust f. Ferat ... 'Hic occisus est apud Forteviot, secundum alios apud Sconam'
858 Death of Kenneth m. Alpin 'rex Pictorum'	(Kenneth) primus Scottorum rexit ... Pictaviam ... quos	Son of the clan of [Áedán] will take the kingdom of	Cinaeth f. Alpin *(Synchr.:* he was the first king of the	

	(i.e. Picts) delevit. Deus enim eos pro merito sue malicie alienos ... hereditate dignatus est facere: qui illi non solum Domini missam ac preceptum spreverunt, sed et in iure equitatis aliis equi parari <n>oluerunt ... Antequam veniret Pictaviam Dalriete regnum suscepit. Septimo anno regni sui reliquias Sancti Columbe transportavit ad ecclesiam quam construxit ... ... Danari vastaverunt Pictaviam	Scotland ('righe Alban'). He is the first king that will reign in the East from among the Erin in Alba ... after violent slaughter. The fierce men in the East are deceived by him ... a deadly pit(?) death by wounding in the middle of Scone of the high shields ... ... Long will it be till his like will come	Gael who possessed the kingdom of Scone)	Kinath m. Alpin ... Super Scotos regnavit, destructis Pictis ... sepultus in Yona ... Hic mira callidate duxit Scotos de Argadia(!) in terram Pictorum
862 Death of Domnall m. Alpin, 'rex Pictorum'	In huius tempore jura ac legis regni Edi f. Ecdach fecerunt Goideli cum rege suo ...		Domnall f. Alpin	... sepultus in Yona
875 Battle of 'Picts' vs. 'dark foreigners', with 'great slaughter' 876 Death of Custantin m. Kenneth 'rex Pictorum'	... vastavit Amlaib cum gentibus suis Pictaviam ... ... bello ... in Dolair inter Danarios et Scottos ... Normanni annum integrum degerunt in Pictavia.	Another young king will take sovereignty the cow-herd of the byre of the cows of the Cruithnech ... three battles will be gained over the heathen ... (five) years as 'Ri Alban'	et Custantin f. Cinæda	... interfectus est a Norwigensibus ... sepultus in Iona
878 Aed m. Kenneth 'rex Pictorum' killed 'a sociis'	Edus ...		Æd f. Cinæda	... interfectus ... a Girg f. Dungal, sep. in Iona
	Eochodius ... Ciricius ...	[positive view of Giric, scathing on Donald twice over]	Giric m. Dungaile	Hic primus dedit libertatem ecclesiæ Scoticanæ quæ sub servitute erat usque ad illum tempus ex constitutione et more Pictorum
900 Death of Domnall m. Constantine, 'ri Alban'.	Donald f. Constantini ... Normanni tum vastaverunt Pictaviam ... ... bellum ... inter Danarios et Scottos		Domnull f. Constantin	
	Constantinus f. Edii ... Normanni predaverunt Duncalden omnemque Albaniam ... ... Ac in vi anno Constantinus rex et	Welcome, welcome if he it is who has long been prophesied ... A fair long reign with fruit, ale, music ... Battles will not	Custantin f. Æda	Hic dimisso regno ... abbas factus Keledeorum S. Andreæ ... et ibi ... sepultus

952 Death of Constantine m. Aed, 'ri Alban'		Cellachus episcopus leges disciplinasque fidei atque iura ecclesiarum ewangeliorumque pariter cum Scottis in colle credulitatis, prope regali civitati Scoan devoverunt custodire	stand against him ... God is faithful to him ...

From The 'Dunkeld Litany'

Ut animalia nostra ab omni lue pestifera custodias ... ... Ut Episcopos, Abbates Kiledeos et omnem populum totius Albaniae, conserves et protegas. Ut regem nostrum Girich cum exercitu suo ab omnibus inimicorum insidiis tuearis et defendas: TE ROGAMUS AUDI NOS.

Notes ~~~~~~

On Tabulated Sources

For reasons given at the outset of the text, it seems important not only to set out as much as possible of the exiguous evidence for the course of events in ninth century northern Britain, but also to bring out the extent to which different sources may have different agenda: hence the use of five columns, except for the entry from the 'Dunkeld Litany', quoted in conclusion.

(i) Col. 1: *Annals of Ulster (AU:* Mac Airt and Mac Niocaill, 1983); I have not cited other witnesses to the 'Chronicle of Ireland' (Hughes, 1972, 99-115; Smyth, 1972; most recently, Grabowski and Dumville, 1984, 111-27), inasmuch as they add little or nothing to what *AU* has to offer on North British matters. Everything we know about *AU* suggests that it may be taken as a contemporary (which is not of course to say objective) record; but this applies only to entries in the main hand, not to glosses or interpolations.

(ii) Col. 2: 'Poppleton Chronicle' (ed. Anderson, 1973, 235-60; see also Anderson, 1949, 31-42). This Chronicle stands in the MS as a continuation of Pictish king-list 'A', one of the 'P' class (cf. (iv) below), with a red-ink initial that marks no more of a break than those denoted by new paragraphs throughout Mrs Anderson's edition, 245-53 - and with less of a break than at the introduction of the Scottish king-list proper (253, n. 161), which is at least launched by a red-ink rubric: cf. the facsimile in Skene, 1867, facing p. 3, also Anderson, 1949, 34-7; accordingly, this column also contains in square brackets entries from the 'A' list after the 780s, retaining MS orthography as reproduced by Mrs Anderson, but omitting the attributed reign-lengths on the grounds that, in principle if not in fact, these are yet more liable to distortion than the order of names. For the unique authority of this source see Cowan, 1981; Miller, 1982, 137-42; and Broun, 1994b; with (forthcoming) a study by John Bannerman, *Studies in the History of Scotia*, and an edition/translation by Ben Hudson. I accept the case that it was compiled (in Gaelic) in the later tenth century from materials that were contemporary for the ninth; if this makes it relatively reliable in the facts it chooses to report, the same cannot necessarily be said for the choice it made, nor for the gloss it put upon them. The *prima facie* conclusion from its final entry is that it was written not only in the reign of Kenneth II (971-95) but also at Brechin. However, there is an obvious case for an Abernethy element among its sources, given its inclusion of two Abernethy 'charters' (Davies, 1982b, 273), only the first of which is shared with lists 'B' and 'C' (col. 4); and it might paradoxically be concluded from the failure to specify that Dunkeld was the new *ecclesia* to which Kenneth Mac Alpin translated St Columba's relics (Macquarrie, 1992, 121-3), that Dunkeld provided another ingredient in the mixture. Less likely is any significant St Andrews contribution. Part of the Poppleton collection probably did originate there, and a whole textual family of the king-list on which it drew has strong St Andrews connections (see col. 5). But the Chronicle's perspectives differ in a number of ways from that set of lists, e.g. in its lack of enthusiasm about Giric (p. 142 above), and its reserve verging on hostility towards Constantine II's side of the dynasty (cf. Hudson, 1994, 91-4) - it does not even mention that Constantine II's retirement was to St Andrews.

(iii) Col. 3: 'Prophecy of Berchan' (ed. in part Skene, 1867, 79-105; tr. Anderson, 1922, I, *passim*, and cf. xxxiv-xxxvi; also Anderson, 1930; a new edition/translation is forthcoming from Ben Hudson). The evidence of this example of Celtic 'back-prophecy' is not to be accepted uncorroborated, even when one can be confident what it means (note the regular discrepancy between Skene and Anderson translations, the latter being quoted here). If it was really composed as late as the 1160s (compare Anderson, 1922, xxxv, with Anderson,

1930, 4), this is unexpected testimony to the persistence of the 'Gaelic' ideology it represents (cf. above, pp. 144).

(iv) Col. 4: this column combines the evidence of the 'Synchronisms' (Thurneysen, 1933; Boyle, 1971) and *'Duan Albanach'* (Jackson, 1957) on the kings of Dal Riata and from Kenneth mac Alpin onwards, with that of the other 'P' class Pictish king-lists, 'B' and 'C' (Anderson, 1973, 261-3; cf. Miller, 1982 146-8, 159-61). It is important (cf. above, p. 136) that the latter continue with no break through Kenneth and down to Malcolm III, and it is the 'B' list that is the major item in this column (again in Anderson's orthography); Dál Riatan kings are entered in Italics, spellings being Boyle's, from the Edinburgh MS of the Synchronisms, and brackets denoting information lacking in one or other versions (these include patronymics, among them the generally discredited notion that Domnall was Constantine's son). The *Duan* and the ancestor of the 'B'/'C' lists appear to date to the reign of Malcolm III, and it seems certain that they share a common source (Anderson, 1973, 48-9). Less certain but not impossible is that this was also the source of the Synchronisms (*ibid*., 44-6); we could thus envisage that a package representing one interpretation of Dál Riatan, Pictish and Scottish royal succession made its way to Ireland in the later eleventh century (cf. *ibid*., 51); though we should then have to reject Mrs Anderson's view that the short version of the Synchronisms, ending with Malcolm II (d. 1034), was the older, as well as their ascription by Skene to Fland Mainistrech (d.1056). It should also be noted that, unlike the *Duan* or even the 'X'/'Y' lists (below, col. 5), shorter and longer Synchronisms each intrude a King Alpin between Eoganan mac Oengusa and the start of the Scottish series proper (Boyle, 1971, 170; Anderson, 1973, 46, n. 10); but their texts seem corrupt in different ways, the former repeating Eoganan and the latter omitting Kenneth himself; this may be further evidence of an adjusted story of the Scots' takeover (above, pp. 135-136, below, col. 5).

(v) Col. 5: here, Mrs Anderson's 'X' class of Dál Riatan and Scottish king-lists (1973, 49-67) is blended with the Pictish lists of her 'Q' class (*ibid*., 84-102): spellings are those of list 'F' (*ibid*., 271-5). It needs to be appreciated that, as is not immediately apparent from her separate discussions, 'Q' lists are invariably incorporated into 'X' lists, usually and perhaps originally between the Dál Riatan kings and Kenneth Mac Alpin; only one 'X' list does not include a 'Q' list, and that in fact starts with Kenneth. Most 'X' lists have a St Andrews connection of sorts (Cowan, 1981, 6-7), and the notice in 'Q' lists of the 'building of St Andrews' by Angus mac Fergus (II) seems to link up with the St Andrews foundation legend; it is reasonable, therefore, to trace the 'X'/'Q' tradition back to that house. As for its date, much depends on the interpretation of Mrs Anderson's 'Y' lists (1973, 49-52, 67-76), a group tending to associate in one way or another with Melrose. This group lacks the notes on each Scottish reign which are the key feature of 'X' lists, and which are partially excerpted in this column; if, as Mrs Anderson argues, they were dropped from the source of the 'Y' lists' rather than added to that of 'X', then they must pre-date the 1160s, when the ancestor of one of the 'Y' lists appears to have become fossilized; otherwise, they could be dated at any time down to Alexander II's reign, when the source of one set of 'X' lists evidently concluded. A significant aspect of both 'X' and 'Y' lists is that they re-arrange the order of Dál Riatan kings, so as to make the Alpin who probably died in the 730s into the immediate predecessor of Kenneth (mac Alpin): that is, once again to convert the Alpin who fathered Kenneth into a king (compare the Synchronisms, above, col. 4). The persistent confusion over this Alpin must tend to discredit the otherwise circumstantial evidence of the 'Chronicle of Huntingdon' (Skene, 1867, 209; Anderson, 1922, 270-1; Anderson, 1973, 194-5; Cowan, 1981, 13-16; Hudson, 1991, 15-17), in that Alpin father of Kenneth is there represented as a king, whose death in battle against the Picts Kenneth went on so spectacularly to avenge; the Huntingdon evidence is therefore omitted from this table.

(vi) The 'Dunkeld Litany' (for its provenance, see Haddan and Stubbs, 1873, 278-85) seems to be an almost entirely unknown quantity, having been ignored since the 1870s until Ben Hudson again drew attention to it (1994, 131) - though cf. McRoberts (1953), no. 81. Professors Archie Duncan and Donald Watt kindly warn me that anything from such a context is to be regarded with the utmost suspicion; yet it is difficult to see that the quoted passages, or some other parts of this litany, are likely to have been invented after the twelfth century.

Bibliography~~~~~~

Airlie, S. 1994, 'The View from Maastricht', in Crawford, 1994, 33-46.

Alcock, L. and E. 1993, 'Reconnaissance excavations on Early Historic fortifications and other royal sites in Scotland, 1974-84; 5:A, Excavations and other fieldwork at Forteviot, Perthshire, 1981, etc.', *Proceedings of the Society of Antiquaries of Scotland,* 122, 215-87.

Anderson, A. 1922, *Early Sources of Scottish History A.D. 500-1286*, 2 vols, Edinburgh.

Anderson, A. 1930, 'The Prophecy of Berchan', *Zeitschrift fir celtische Philologie* xviii, 1-56.

Anderson, M. 1949, 'The Scottish Materials in the Paris Manuscript, Bib. Nat., Latin 4126', *Scottish Historical Review* xxviii, 31-42.

Anderson, A. and M. 1961, *Adomnan's Life of Columba*, Edinburgh.

Anderson, M. 1973, *Kings and Kingship in Early Scotland*, Edinburgh.

Anderson, M. 1982, 'Dalriada and the creation of the kingdom of the Scots', in Whitelock *et al.*, 1982, 106-32.

Bannerman, J. 1971, 'The Scots of Dalriada', in G. Menzies (ed.), *Who are the Scots*?, London, 66-79.

Bannerman, J. 1974, *Studies in the History of Dalriada*, Edinburgh.

Bartlett, R. 1993, *The Making of Europe. Conquest, Colonization and Cultural Change 950-1350*, Harmondworth.

Blake, E. 1962, *Liber Eliensis*, London, Camden Society, 3rd ser. xcii.

Boyle, A. 1971, 'The Edinburgh Synchronisms of Irish Kings', *Celtica* ix, 169-75.

Brooks, N. 1984, *The Early History of the Church of Canterbury*, Leicester, Studies in the Early History of Britain.

Broun, D. 1994a, 'The Origin of Scottish Identity in its European Context', in Crawford, 1994, 21-31.

Broun, D. 1994b, 'The Origin of Scottish Identity', in C. Bjørn, A. Grant and K. Stringer (eds), *Nations, Nationalism and Patriotism in the European Past,* Copenhagen, 35-55.

Byrne, F-J. 1973, *Irish Kings and High-Kings*, London.

Chadwick, H. 1949, *Early Scotland*, Cambridge.

Charles-Edwards, T.M. 1995, 'Language and Society among the Insular Celts AD 400-1000', in M.J. Green (ed.), *The Celtic World*, London.

Cowan, E. 1981, 'The Scottish Chronicle in the Poppleton Manuscript', *Innes Review* xxxii, 3-21.

Cowan, I. 1974, 'The Post-Columban Church', *Proceedings of the Church History Society of Scotland* 8, 245-60.

Crawford, B. 1994, *Scotland in Dark Age Europe*, St Andrews, St John's House Papers no. 5.

Davies, W. 1982a, *Wales in the Early Middle Ages*, Leicester, Studies in the Early History of Britain.

Davies, W. 1982b, 'The Latin charter-tradition in western Britain, Brittany and Ireland in the early mediaeval period', in Whitelock *et al.*, 1982, 258-80.

Davies, W. 1990, *Patterns of Power in Early Wales*, Oxford.

Davies, R. 1990, *Domination and Conquest. The experience of Ireland, Scotland and Wales, 1100-1300,* Cambridge.

Dumville, D. 1977a, 'Kingship, Genealogies and Regnal Lists', in Sawyer and Wood, 1977, 72-104.

Dumville, D. 1977b, 'Sub-Roman Britain: History and Legend', *History* 62, 173-92.

Duncan, A. 1975, *Scotland: the Making of the Kingdom*, Edinburgh History of Scotland I.

Duncan, A. 1981, 'Bede, Iona and the Picts', in R.H.C. Davis and J.M. Wallace-Hadrill (eds), *The Writing of History in the Middle Ages. Essays Presented to Richard William Southern*, Oxford, 1-42.

Duncan, A. 1993, 'The Laws of Malcolm MacKenneth', in A. Grant and K. Stringer (eds), *Medieval Scotland. Crown, Lordship and Community*, Edinburgh, 239-73.

Forsyth, K. 1995, 'The Inscriptions on the Dupplin Cross', *From the Isles of the North: Medieval Art in Ireland and Britain (Proceedings of the Third International Conference on Insular Art)* Belfast, 237-44.

Forsyth, K. 1996, *Language in Pictland: the case against non-Indo-European Pictish,* Van Hamel lecture, Utrecht.

Frame, R. *The Political Development of the British Isles*, 1100-1400, Oxford.

Grabowski, K. and Dumville, D. 1984, *Chronicles and Annals of Mediaeval Ireland and Wales,* Woodbridge, Studies in Celtic History IV.

Greene, D. 1972. Review of K. Jackson, *The Gaelic Notes in the Book of Deer, Studia Hibernica* 12, 167-70.

Greene, D. 1983, 'Gaelic: syntax, similarities with British syntax', in D. Thomson (ed.), *Companion to Gaelic Scotland*, Oxford, 107-8.

Haddan, A. and Stubbs, W. 1873, *Councils and Ecclesiastical Documents relating to Great Britain and Ireland,* 3 vols, Oxford (vol. II).

Hamilton, N. 1870, *William of Malmesbury, Gesta Pontificum Anglorum*, London, Rolls Series 52.

Heather, P. 1994, 'State Formation in Europe in the First Millenium A.D.', in Crawford, 1994, 47-70.

Henderson, I. 1967, *The Picts*, London.

Hudson, B. 1994, *Kings of Celtic Scotland*, Westport, Connecticut.

Hudson, B. 1991, 'The Conquest of the Picts in Early Scottish Literature', *Scottish Studies* xv, 13-25.

Hughes, K. 1972, *Early Christian Ireland: Introduction to the Sources*, Cambridge.

Hughes, K. 1980, 'Where are the writings of early Scotland?', in K. Hughes and D. Dumville (eds), *Celtic Britain in the Early Middle Ages*, Woodbridge, Studies in Celtic History II, 1-21.

Jackson, K. 1955, 'The Pictish Language', in F. Wainwright (ed.), *The Problem of the Picts,* Edinburgh, 129-66.

Jackson, K. 1957, 'The Duan Albanach', *Scottish Historical Review* xxxvi, 125-37.

Jenkins, D. 1986, *Hywel Dda, The Law*, Llandysul, Welsh Classics 2.

Kenney, J. 1929, *The Sources for the Early History of Ireland: Ecclesiastical*, New York.

Keynes, S. and Lapidge, M. 1983, *Alfred the Great*, Harmondsworth.

Mac Airt, S. 1951, *The Annals of Inisfallen*, Dublin, Institute for Advanced Studies.

Mac Airt, S. and Mac Niocaill, G. 1983, *The Annals of Ulster (to A.D. 1131)*, Dublin, Institute for Advanced Studies.

Macaulay, D. 1975, Review of K. Jackson, *The Gaelic Notes in the Book of Deer, Scottish Historical Review* liv, 64-7.

Macquarrie, A. 1990, 'Early Christian Govan: the Historical Context', *Proceedings of the Church History Society of Scotland* 24, 1-17.

Macquarrie, A. 1992, 'Early Christian religious houses in Scotland: foundation and function', in J. Blair and R. Sharpe (eds), *Pastoral Care Before the Parish*, Leicester, 110-33.

McKitterick, R. 1977, *The Frankish Church and the Carolingian Reforms, 789-895*, London, Royal Historical Society.

Maitland, F. 1897, *Domesday Book and Beyond*, Cambridge.

Miller, M. 1982, 'Matriliny by treaty: the Pictish foundation-legend', in Whitelock *et al.*, 1982, 133-61.

Morris, J. 1980, *Nennius. British History and the Welsh Annals*, Chichester, Arthurian Period Sources 8.

O'Brien, M. 1962, *Corpus Genealogiorum Hiberniae* (vol. I), Dublin, Institute for Advanced Studies.

Ó'Corráin, D. 1972, *Ireland before the Normans*, Dublin, Gill History of Ireland 2.

Ó'Corráin, D. 1974, 'Nationality and Kingship in pre-Norman Ireland', in T.W. Moody (ed.), *Nationality and the Pursuit of National Independence*, Belfast, Historical Studies XI, 1-35.

Ó'Riain, P. 1990, 'A misunderstood Annal: a hitherto unnoticed Cáin', *Celtica* xxii, 561-6.

Pohl, W. 1988, *Die Awaren. Ein Steppenvolk in Mitteleuropa 567-822*, Munich.

Reuter, T. 1985, 'Plunder and Tribute in the Carolingian Empire', *Transactions of the Royal Historical Society,* 5th ser. 35 (1985), 75-94.

Reuter, T. 1990, ‘The End of Carolingian Military Expansion’, in P. Godman and R. Collins (eds), *Charlemagne’s Heir. New Perspectives on the Reign of Louis the Pious (814-840),* 391-405.

Rollason, D. 1989, *Saints and Relics in Anglo-Saxon England*, Oxford.

Sawyer. P. and Wood, I. 1977, *Early Medieval Kingship*, Leeds.

Scharer, A. 1996, ‘The Anglo-Saxon Chronicle, Asser’s Life of Alfred, and the Writing of History at Alfred’s Court’, *Early Medieval Europe* 5

Sellar, W.D.H. 1985, ‘Warlords, Holy Men and Matrilineal Succession’, *Innes Review* xxxvi, 29-43.

Skene, W. 1867, *Chronicles of the Picts, Chronicles of the Scots, and other Early Memorials of Scottish History,* Edinburgh.

Skene, W. 1876, *Celtic Scotland: A History of Ancient Alban*, 3 vols, Edinburgh.

Smyth, A. 1972, ‘The earliest Irish Annals: their first contemporary entries, and the earliest centuries of recording’, *Proceedings of the Royal Irish Academy* 72C(i), 1-48.

Smyth, A. 1984, *Warlords and Holy Men*, London, The New History of Scotland 1.

Todd, J. 1867, *The War of the Gaedhil with the Gaill*, London, Rolls Series 48.

Thomas, C. 1961, ‘The Animal Art of the Scottish Iron Age and its Origins’, *Archaeological Journal* cxviii, 14-64.

Thomas, C. 1963, ‘The Interpretation of the Pictish Symbols’, *Archaeological Journal* cxx, 31-97.

Thurneysen, R. 1933, ‘Synchronismen der Irischen Kønige’, *Zeitschrift für celtische Philologie* xix, 81-99.

Ullmann, W. 1969, *The Carolingian Renaissance and the Idea of Kingship*, London.

Wallace-Hadrill, M. 1971, *Early Germanic Kingship in England and on the Continent*, Oxford.

Watson, W.J. 1926, *The History of the Celtic Place-Names of Scotland*, Edinburgh

Whitelock, D. *English Historical Documents (vol. I), c. 500-1042*, 2nd edn, 1979.

Whitelock, D., McKitterick, R. and Dumville, D. 1982, *Ireland in Early Mediaeval Europe. Studies in Memory of Kathleen Hughes,* Cambridge.

Wickham, C. 1981, *Early Medieval Italy. Central Power and Local Society 400-1000,* London.

Williams, I. 1982, *Armes Prydein: The Prophecy of Britain*, Dublin, Institute for Advanced Studies.

Wormald, P. 1977, '*Lex Scripta* and *Verbum Regis:* Legislation and Germanic Kingship from Euric to Cnut', in Sawyer and Wood, 1977, 105-38.

Wormald, P. 1986, 'Celtic and Anglo-Saxon Kingship: some further thoughts', in P. Szarmach and V. Oggins (eds), *Sources of Anglo-Saxon Culture*, Kalamazoo, Studies in Medieval Culture XX, 151-83.

Wormald, P. 1994, '*Engla Lond:* the Making of an Allegiance', *Journal of Historical Sociology* 7, 1-24.

JAMES THIN Ltd
1898218617

3 ALL CARDS TOT: #9.00
AMT: #9.00
#9.00
REC: 155966:240296:1508:30sports
*** THANK YOU, COME AGAIN ***